Metal
Never Lies

An Introduction to Metal Magic

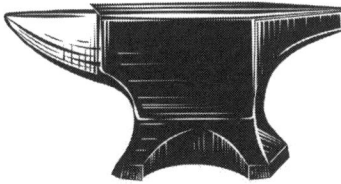

SAM 'BO' THOMPSON

Metal Never Lies

Copyright © 2022 by Sam Thompson

All Rights Reserved.

Disclaimer

Every effort has been made to trace or contact all copyright holders. The publishers will be pleased to make good any omissions or rectify any mistakes brought to their attention at the earliest opportunity.

This book does not replace the advice of a medical professional. Consult your physician before making any changes to your diet or regular health plan.

ISBN 979-8-9866825-1-8 Paperback

ISBN 979-8-9866825-0-1 Ebook

Thompson Consulting

www.RavensKeepForge.com

Dedication

I dedicate this book to my Beloved, Julie.
Without her cheerleading, constant support,
valuable advice, and her immense amount of
love, this book would not be. She is the Moon to
my Sun and makes my world work.

Contents

Part 1: Foundation 7

What Is Metal Magic? 14

Animistic Thinking............................... 19

Blood and Bones 21

A Tool and a Weapon...........................23

Types of Metal.....................................26

Copper 28

Bronze 31

Brass 33

Iron and Steel.....................................35

Acquire 38

Summary of Part 1 42

Part 2: The Rabbit Hole 43

If…,Then…. 46

Lore...48

Possibilities 58

Other Traditions' Use of Metal and Magical
Weapons 61

Magical metal workers......................63

Summary of Part 2 65

Part 3: F.L.O.W.......................**67**

Don't Want to Make Your Own? 70

Repurpose, Reclaim, Upcycle 72

Relationship......................75

Feel 77

Listen......................80

Open......................84

Metal Meditation 87

Work......................90

Use What You Have 93

The Blade or That's What She Said 94

Weekend Workshops......................100

Summary of Part 3 102

Part 4: Tools, Projects & Rituals **105**

"Got to Have" Tools 107

Nice To Have Tools 115

Splurge-able Tools 117

Project Inception......................120

INCITE......................121

Projects 128

Design Ideas 129

Something Different 140

Ritual 141

Activating the Metal Magic 144

Some Possible Additions to Ritual 146

Summary of Part 4 153

Introduction

Despite their obvious metallic coldness, each item felt warm to me, an old warmth, like I'd been holding it for a while already. May seem odd, but an instant, old connection if you will. Nicholas S

This book is written for those who yearn to add something more to their magical and spiritual lives. They have that itch that knows there is something missing. They are the type that aren't afraid of putting in some time and effort to do some Work. They will roll up their sleeves to experiment and explore something new, yet ancient. This book answers the question: How can I incorporate Metal Magic into my Spiritual practice?

Within these pages readers will examine parts of history as seen in Irish mythology on metal magic, immerse themselves in and understand the properties of several common metals, explore current uses and ponder ways to incorporate metal magic into daily life.

Along the way the reader will create projects to aid them in their work. Upon completion of the activities, the participant should feel confident to include metals magically on a regular basis and be resolute in the knowledge acquired of both the metal and of themselves. They will be capable of impactful metal work.

This book is unique in several ways. It is written by a magical blacksmith, who has shipped magical metal items over much of the world. One who currently teaches the craft of blacksmithing in a primitive method as well as metal magic. My background is more with the Irish lore so I will have a heavy slant to that mythology. This book has been specifically designed so you can learn magical metal work with limited tools (or possibly none at all) that most will have on hand or can easily find. It is my goal that you spend your time doing the Work, not collecting gadgets and doodads. There will be a heavy focus on copper and steel. It is what I have the most familiarity with, and they are also fairly readily available. These metals have been around since, I don't know, the copper and iron age maybe. I will also talk about brass and bronze. I work with them as well, although in a different fashion as you will discover. Are you ready?

As "connected" as we have become in the modern world, I believe in doing so, we have also become disconnected from a very important part of ourselves. Most of us are surrounded by metal all day, every day, yet it goes unnoticed. I bet it's safe to say that there are a few who don't even really see it. We have become numb to it. Cut ourselves off from it, even if by accident. And in doing so, it is my belief that we've also cut off an important part of us. In the midst of a pandemic many of us have become tired, almost lifeless, lacking motivation and maybe even will. To me this is the perfect time to turn to a valuable ally we have easily within our reach, the magic of metal!

I have no doubt that some of the lack of using metal magic, is because there really is not much information 'out there' on this subject. I know I have looked for it, (I may have very well looked in the wrong places, who knows, and the internet is a scary place these days). I also think not knowing how to work with metal can be a big deterrent from using it. Which leads to, how does one use it and just what are the 'properties' of it, really? If you don't know the properties and you don't know how to work with it, how on earth can you possibly build a relationship with it? And if you don't know the properties or how to work with it, and you can't really create a relationship with it, how could you even fathom the idea of creating tools with metal to use in your magical practice? This is what we are going to fix, together. And what makes me say this? I've done it. I have taught people about these very things for years. People who have no experience in metal working. You don't need to be a blacksmith or a metal worker to make metal items for magical uses. And I will show you how.

For me personally, one of the big benefits of metal magic is the re-connection. It has become a re-awakening of myself. A realization of a missing puzzle piece that fit right in. The world around me has a different hum or vibration to it. To me it's palpable. There is now an additional level of energy. It has altered the way I see life around me. It is as if the world has become more connected, more accessible. Metal magic isn't something new. It has always been there. I just wasn't paying much attention to it.

Then there is the crafting side, what I refer to as co-creating. I find it exhilarating to be in a position to be able to feel and listen to the metal, then be able to work on the practice of metal magic itself. It has become my lifestyle, creating metal items magically. It's a completely new and wonderful existence. A world full of life, knowledge and wisdom.

Reconnecting with metal can lead to experiencing life differently. Metals are very much a part of the natural world we live in. We will do some simple exercises that will help you have a much deeper understanding of the metals that surround you today. You will learn multiple ways to build relationships with metal. It will no longer be an inanimate object to you. You will have the opportunity to create some powerful magical items with metals. Simply taking the time to learn metal magic, it will be a great addition to your current magical practice. It will open a whole new world of potential for you. You quite possibly will never be the same again.

Here is the journey that I have laid out before you. Think of me as being your facilitator, or guide as you start to understand and appreciate this new practice. The first thing we are going to do is lay a foundation. We'll define what metal magic is, discuss multiple ways to add it into our practice. We will also take a look at the difference between tool vs weapon. Then we are going to lay out some thoughts on the different types of metal, specifically steel, bronze, brass, and copper. After we have a good foundation, the real fun begins. (Of course, this will depend on your definition of fun I suppose.) We are going to look at some Irish mythology that got this whole metal magic thing really going for me. Maybe I will even help connect some dots that could very well take you down a rabbit hole of epic proportions. It has for me.

Next, I am going to lay out a method that I teach that has been easy to remember and apply to working with metal. Since some of you will want to try your hand at making some magical items, I will give you a list of need-to-have and nice-to-have tools as we start some simple projects. Most of the needed tools you may very well have on hand. Don't panic if you don't want to craft your own items. This method will be easy to apply to metal items you already have as well.

One of the most important bits is safety. Please be safe, physically and energetically. I will explain some projects you should be able to do in your own space, no matter where you are. Sprinkled in along our adventure, I am going to add in a few perspectives from those who have commissioned some of my Work, as well as those who have traveled here to take a weekend Immersion with me. I think it is important that you hear from others, as their words may be of help and resonate with you.

I would like to offer this prayer to my Goddess the Morrigan as we start our journey:

Morrigan, Great Queen

I am grateful to be in service to you.

May I speak my truth with courage and compassion.

Morrigan Great Queen

I am grateful for my Work.

May I serve you with honor and integrity.

Morrigan, Great Queen

I am grateful for my ability.

May I have the wisdom and strength to flourish.

So be it.

Part 1

Foundation

First and foremost, these are my experiences. The information and ideas that follow are what I have learned and what I currently use as I understand it. As a Magical Blacksmith and Priest of the Morrigan, I see a big part of my Work as providing tools so others can do their Work. (I have 'work' capitalized because of what it is- I think of it as that thing one does in service to their Deity, or that thing that is their Purpose.)

OK, enough of all that.

This is how I see Metal Magic. It is the use of metals to aid in your Work. There are a lot of metal items I think that are overlooked. How about the modern wedding or handfasting ring for instance? These are oath rings, a type of binding magic. There are many ways to use what is referred to as precious metals in your Work. I wear a silver torc around my neck that was created by a sacred silversmith. I put it on at the time of my dedication to the Morrigan; I have not taken it off since. To me, it is a symbol of my oath and a reminder of my Work. I have no doubt that my Beloved uses metal magic in the kitchen. Think of the pans, pots, knives, utensils, etc. Not only to create tasty meals but also for health and wellbeing.

-**Action step**: Take a moment and inventory what is around your everyday environment that is metal. Everything. Pots, pans, coins, knives, tools, keys etc. Get up, walk around and look if you must. Write it down. This will be of use later to you. My goal in this is to get you thinking about how to incorporate metal magic into your daily Work.

Before we get too far along, let me unpack this word 'tool' for a moment and what I mean when I use it. Merriam-Webster defines a tool as *'a handheld device that aids in accomplishing a task'*. It can be a hammer, pliers, or saw, as well as an athame, wand, fire striker and even an incense holder.

To me, metals have their own energy, or life/spirit. Some are big and robust; others are small and quiet. There are some metal items that are even asleep. Intent is inherent within the tool and is compounded by *our own intention* for the use of the tool. I say this from my own experience at the smithy. There are times I will grab a piece of metal and think, 'I need you to be this', and other times I will wander around saying, 'I need to create this, who wants to be it?' It really depends on what I am making. If my aim is to create a magical tool, I lean heavily on the asking. I ask a lot!

One morning my Beloved and I were talking about metal magic. As we discussed it, she said it was something she never really thought much about, and this is from someone who designs wire wrapped jewelry. She said she does think about the properties of the different wire, and that's about it. We talked about times we've shopped at the local new age shop for a magical tool. What did we find? Crystals. Lots and lots of crystals. And candles. Don't think that I am anti-crystal or candle; I'm not. I just think there's such a great opportunity to add metal to the mix! You can buy a crystal or candle for xyz purposes, or you can create a metal tool for the same purpose. I vote let's make it!

There are probably some of you that are thinking, 'well gee whiz, Bo, all that sounds lovely and all, but I'm not a blacksmith. I can't forge items. It's just so much easier to go buy something.' And you know what- you are partly right. It IS easier to go buy something. After all, it's your process. You do you. Or you could find yourself a blacksmith to work with you (depending on what you want to make, this could be the direction you want to go). Another choice is to create it yourself. 'Create' can mean starting from scratch OR using what you already have. This is what I want to help you do. Find something you have, build a relationship with it and put it to use. Will it be easy? Maybe. Probably not. It reminds me of that quote from the movie A League of

Their Own. "It's supposed to be hard. If it wasn't hard, everyone would do it. The hard is what makes it great."

So, metal magic is using metal to help support you with a desired effect. As we looked at it being a tool, I think it can also be used as a weapon. It doesn't need to be a sharp, shiny pointy thing. Another definition from Merriam-Webster, to make sure we are on the same page: *Weapon - Any instrument or device for use in attack or defense.* (Not solely from people- it expands to energy as well.)

Sometimes I find my worst enemy can be myself doing that 'stinking thinking'. I don't know about you, but sometimes I am doing battle with what I call a death spiral of depression or sadness. Using some form of iron or steel for strength and stamina works for me, helps with that warding. A pendant or a pocket notion works nicely. Steel has some heft to it; with it in my pocket, I am reminded throughout the day to refocus on what I need to whenever I notice it in my pocket. A copper bracelet works well to add a little pep to my daily step so to speak. Copper also really helps with energy flow and can be healing. We'll get into more of the properties directly.

Giving a bit of background information may add some color to the overall story. I call the southern Appalachian Mountains home. Specifically, Western North Carolina. All my family is from East Tennessee. I don't currently live in either place; my home is in the Foothills of NC. Anyway, I still remember my granddad fondly, and him having a smithy in his 'workshop'. Most folks did. At that time people fixed the tools that they had. I remember asking him why he didn't just go buy another one. He said it was because he was able to fix it. The only time you go buy a new one is when you can't fix or make do with what you have. That was an early life lesson, and it has really stuck with me to this day. Now, I have spent my fair share of time buying shiny new stuff. But the older I get, the more I understand the immense value of his point of view. Looking back on my childhood now, I can see how some outside people may think that we didn't live as neat and tidy as some others. They may have seen some 'junk' lying around. We knew where everything was. My father-in-law used to say, you never know when you may need that. A truer statement has never been said! To us it wasn't junk. It was future tools or items that would be needed. My smithy is like this now, for the most part. I would say that 98% or so is reclaimed metal - junk to most. I do know where most of it came from; it all has a story to me. I think this is an important part- the history of it.

Back to my granddad- he's the reason I got into blacksmithing in the first place. He crossed over some time ago. I felt the need to do something to honor him and the memories I have of him. I fondly remember him saying you fix what you have. You make do and make it work. With this in mind, smithing seemed like a good place as any to start. I think I did what most people do when they are trying to find out about something they know nothing about- I went to the internet for information. And was I ever surprised! I mean, how hard could it be, really? Then I saw the price of forging hammers and tongs and anvils and started thinking that maybe I will find another way to honor him. They are really proud of that stuff! And I hadn't even got to the learning part of it yet. Not long after, I ran across a weeklong class held in the NC mountains on primitive blacksmithing- literally using a hole in the ground and simple cheap tools. Bingo! Right up my alley.

The rest, as they say, is history. I brought the knowledge I learned there back home and continued the craft. Little by little I worked on upgrading the forge. Then the smithy. Then my tools. All while working on my skills. Studying and reading what I could find. I started selling some of the stuff I made here and there and doing demo's at festivals just for fun. People asked me to teach them. After a lot of discussion with my Beloved and several more years I did just that, which has enabled me to spend more time smithing and then upgrade tools when I could and as needed.

The next step in my growth came several years back. I started focusing more on the magic of metal. Playing with it, experimenting with it, feeling it, shaping it and understanding it. Back to the internet I went to find out more on magical metal. *Nada.* I didn't really find anything that was of much use to me. No real explanations. There were a few things on the properties of metal, but nothing really on the magic of it. (There is a difference to me.) About this time, I was also in a deep study of The Morrigan and the Irish lore surrounding Her (I'm still very much in a deep study to be honest). She has asked ('politely suggested' for those who understand) that I write this book you now have in your possession. It will have an Irish slant to it as we discuss some of the background and lore, since it is the material I am most familiar with and with which I have an intimate working knowledge. I will be referring to it to bring to light potential and possibility. I will also briefly discuss some other lore from different cultures. Together we will explore opportunities to add metal magic into your life. I want you to think of this as a resource to refer back to. I will give some examples of the process that I go through in working with metal magic. I also hope you understand that this is going to require something of you, the reader. You are going to need to put in some time, thought, effort and possibly a little money to add this into your life (although we'll focus on ways to keep it as inexpensive as possible with lots of alternatives). It really depends on how deeply you want to go, what type of practice you want to build. In my experience, a practice takes time.

A few things to keep in mind: Some of the thoughts or ideas presented may seem a little awkward at first. I ask that you try it the way I have presented it. I know it works. I have been teaching it this way for years with great success. Keep an open mind and let the metal Work come to you. There will be parts that you may find hard. It's ok. It's expected. It's part of the Work. But have fun with it. You will get out of this what you put into it. As with anything worthwhile, it takes practice. It is my desire that you will do the work, to add this into your Work. Let's get to it then!

What Is Metal Magic?

Metal magic is, well, using metal to magically aid you in some way. Seems simple enough. And yet, I have found it to not be necessarily the case. Metal magic has unveiled itself to me as a complete and separate discipline, a path if you would. I have been amazed with its richness and complexity on a level with nothing I have previously experienced. Metal very much has a life of its own. Irish myth speaks to this as we'll discuss in a later section. It is vibrant and unmistakable. Alive.

Think about it: Metal - It's a building block of who we are. Our bodies need iron and copper to function, to live. In a real way, it's an extension of us. Other trace metals too. Tin (added to copper is basically bronze) and zinc (added to copper is basically brass). We have some pretty nifty stuff running around inside us. I knew this, I just didn't KNOW it. Once that puzzle piece dropped in, boom! It's been on!

In this first chapter we will look at ways we can and do use metal in our lives. It is extremely important to have a solid foundation on which to build a practice on. The first is as a magical *tool*. I am going to pause right here. I am a big believer that words mean stuff, so as I go along, I will add definitions to some words as I want to ensure we are using the same frame of reference. As mentioned before, with tools I am referring to a handheld device that aids in conducting a task. Second, metal can very much be used as a *weapon*. As a reminder, by weapon I am referring to it as a means used to defend against or defeat another. Don't limit it to only people. The world is a pretty big place. And yes, metal can be both, tool and a weapon. As we get into the Work, it's important that you understand that metal weapons don't have to be pointy things. There is so much more to metal than that. I believe in the idea that all things—animate and inanimate—have a spirit or an essence, energy if you will. The hills are alive! To me, metals are the blood and bones of the earth.

And speaking of foundation, here is some basic terminology that you should know heading into the rest of the book. Some of these terms are used in the book, others are common terms used for your clarification on terminology and process. This will help you if you want to expand your knowledge outside of this book. This is by no means an exhaustive list, but it will be a good start for you. (1)

Ferrous Metal - Ferrous metals include steel and pig iron (with a carbon content of a few percent) and alloys of iron with other metals (such as stainless steel).

Non-Ferrous Metal - used to describe metals and alloys that do not contain an appreciable amount of iron.

Alloy Metal - a mixture of chemical elements of which at least one is a metal.

Base Metal - distinguished by oxidizing or corroding relatively easily. Examples include iron, nickel, lead, zinc and copper.

Charcoal - Charcoal is a lightweight black carbon residue produced by strongly heating wood (or other animal and plant materials) in minimal oxygen to remove all water and volatile constituents.

Forging - a manufacturing process involving the shaping of metal using localized compressive forces. The blows are delivered with a hammer or die. Forging is one of the oldest known metalworking processes.

Engraving - the practice of incising a design onto a hard, usually flat surface by cutting grooves into it.

Embossing - the material is stretched into a shallow depression. Used primarily for adding decorative patterns.

Wire wrapping - one of the oldest techniques for making handmade jewelry. This technique is done with jewelry wire and findings similar to wire (for example, head-pins) to make components. Wire components are then connected to one another using mechanical techniques with no soldering or heating of the wire.

Filing - helps achieve workpiece function by removing some excess material and deburring the surface.

Annealing - a heat treatment that alters the physical and sometimes chemical properties of a material to increase its ductility and reduce its hardness, making it more workable. It involves heating a material above its recrystallization temperature, maintaining a suitable temperature for an appropriate amount of time and then cooling.

Tempering - process of heat treating, which is used to increase the toughness of iron-based alloys. The various colors produced indicate the temperature to which the steel was heated.

Hardening - process used to increase the hardness of a metal.

Quenching - the rapid cooling of a workpiece in water, oil or air to obtain certain material properties.

Sealing - blocking the passage of fluids through the surface or joints or openings in materials.

Patina - a thin layer that variously forms on the surface of copper, brass, bronze and similar metals (tarnish produced by oxidation or other chemical processes). Patinas can provide a protective covering to materials that would otherwise be damaged by corrosion or weathering.

Casting - a process in which a liquid metal is delivered into a mold (usually by a crucible) that contains a negative impression (i.e., a three-dimensional negative image) of the intended shape.

Anvil – a metalworking tool consisting of a large block of metal (usually forged or cast steel), with a flattened top surface, upon which another object is struck (or "worked").

Vise - a mechanical apparatus used to secure an object to allow work to be performed on it.

Tongs - a type of tool used to grip and lift objects instead of holding them directly with hands.

Chisel - a tool with a characteristically shaped cutting edge of blade on its end, for carving or cutting a hard material such as wood, stone, or metal by hand, struck with a mallet, or mechanical power.

Torch - a tool normally used for the application of flame or heat which uses propane, a hydrocarbon gas, for its fuel and ambient air as its combustion medium.

Eye Protection - protective gear for the eyes, and sometimes face, designed to reduce the risk of injury.

Apron - a functional accessory that protects clothes and skin from stains and marks.

Gloves - protect and comfort hands against cold or heat, damage by friction, abrasion or chemicals, and disease; or in turn to provide a guard for what a bare hand should not touch.

Animistic Thinking

The energy radiating from them (Land Wards)
when I held them in my hands was amazing,
almost like they were vibrating in my hands! I felt
instantly connected to them, like home, safe and
comfortable. Angie C

Since I just brought it up, let us begin with looking at this from an Animistic point of view. Animism(2) is the belief that objects, places, and creatures all possess a distinct spiritual essence. I believe there is 'energy' in the natural world around me. It's a life force, some say it's a vibration. I try to keep in tune with this. The trees and plants are beings, along with the stones. We live together; I am simply a caretaker on this land. We are in a partnership. As far as the metal goes, I passionately believe it has a life of its own. I have spent enough time with it to understand that it can and does communicate. I have the expectation that with practice, you will get to the point of experiencing this for yourself, which will be enormously important going forward if you continue down this path. This belief will help propel your capability to use metal in an effective, magical way.

Action step - Exercise time! I really hope you didn't get this book to just read it. I think you wanted to experience what this metal magic is really all about. You will hear me say this multiple times throughout the book: You will get out of this in direct proportion to what you put into it. This is part of your investment into your practice, part of the Work. So, here it is. Take an inventory of the items around you in your home that you have a magical or deeply emotional connection with. Think of this as a brain dump, do it quickly. Feel free to get up and wander about. This is your list, so put what is important to you. Things can either be out in the open or hidden. Do you have one of those places that you walk by and you know that something special is there without even looking? Your list can be short or long, no matter.

Now that you have your list, write beside each item what they are made of/from. Do your best. We'll come back to it later.

Blood and Bones

...I have felt a huge difference towards iron and copper, especially hand forged pieces. They feel different, stronger, more alive. The energy that forged pieces hold, the magic that I feel from it, is so soothing. Sage W

Two of the metals that we will be working with primarily are copper and iron (or steel). I see these two metals as the blood and bones of the earth. Copper has that "flowy" feel to it; it almost resonates liquid to me. Not a watery liquid, but thick, oozy. Even the color, when tempered correctly (I call this 'flame kissing'), looks like fresh blood to me. It is vibrant. It can also be polished up to an almost mirror finish, a still-water reflection type, even scrying-worthy. Iron, however, has an almost aloof feeling, like it is trying to keep its distance at first. I am sure you have heard the term 'cold as steel.' It also has a strong and rigid energy- dependable, trustworthy. Ever see those pictures of a skyscraper in the beginning stages from back in the 1920's and 1930's? Seems like those fellas were just walking along those beams like it's nothing at all, carrying a lunch bucket. All that foundation is steel. Those buildings are all built upon and around those steel beams. Those are the very bones of the building. The rest of the materials are wrapped around these steel beams. We are going to explore these two specific metals in more detail later. And we will also add in brass and bronze for good measure.

Action Step - Looking at the list that you made earlier, are any of the things you recorded iron/steel, copper, brass or bronze or any other metal? Group these items together by metal type on a different page.

A Tool and a Weapon

I am going to combine both tool and weapon in this section. In my mind there are some blurry lines with these two. Just a reminder: Tool – *a handheld device that aids in carrying out a task.* Weapon - *a means used to defend against or defeat another.*

As I said earlier, not all weapons need to be sharp pointy things. For example, I have 'boundary' markers or wards around my home and The Morrigan's smithy. I see these very much as weapons. In fact, I know they are. They are specifically for defensive, protective measures. How about an athame? I see that as more of a tool than I do a weapon, but it can be both. We could be at this all day. Tomato – Tomato ('Tom-ay-to' or 'Tom-ah-to' - or even 'mater'). I am going to leave it up to you as to how you classify a tool, a weapon or both. It is your list, after all.

There are a lot of ways to add metal into your daily magical life, or just plain ole life for some of us. For uses on my altar, I have crafted items such as candle plate, altar plate, offering dish, offering cup, statuary base (I made a base of spears that my Morrigan statue sits on), athame, wand, incense holders, anvil dust, black salt, divination die, Fionn's Window, my Ogham set, a binding knot and I am sure there will be more as time passes. Now, please don't think that I have ALL of this on my altar at one time; it would be rather crowded. Each does get used from time to time though, as I feel is right as to the Work I am doing. Looking at the list of items I just gave you, which would you say are tools and which ones would you say are weapons?

What about EDC (Everyday Carry)? I will admit that I do not have much in this area. Most of the time all I have on my person is a pocket notion, bracelet, pendant, my handfasting ring and of course my torc. In my life, I do not generally go far from Her smithy. I pretty much live and work here, on this land. And in the smithy, it kind of rattles and hums most of the time with all the different metals in there, so I usually keep it to a minimum personally. I know others will include weaponry of some form on their person. I think most will have a set of keys which can be 'weaponized'. They can be used for personal protection as well as the defense of 'locking' up your residence. What is in your EDC list? Are there any tools or weapons? Can they be made into them?

Action Step - Looking at your grouping of metal items that you first made, how do you think you can use some of them magically? Feel free to get creative with it, there is no rush. And while you are at it, would you classify each item as a tool or weapon? This may be important later. Just sayin'.

By now I hope you've come to an understanding that metal magic is in a way, just an extension of you. It is a physical part of you. That it has its own energy, vibration, or life force. We have touched on a few of the metals that we will primarily be working with in this book, steel, copper, brass, and bronze. Hopefully, you have an awareness of how tools and weapons will be used by me and more importantly, how you are going to refer to items going forward. You have refined your lists, and probably even added to them. By doing this, you should be able to see a significant opportunity to add in metal, in a magical way, to your daily life. Without even collecting more 'stuff'.

Let's have a look at these metals in more practical detail, and a few ideas as to where to find them.

Types of Metal

Now that I have had the experience of working with both copper and iron, I can say each has its own energy and personality. Phoenix D

In the following we will discuss the more commonplace properties of copper, brass, bronze and steel. I don't plan on spending a lot of time or going in much depth on this part. If you have access to the internet, a quick search will give you plenty of information on metal properties with some myths and lore from various cultures. I am going to focus primarily on the ones that I have an intimate working knowledge of. As we go through this discovery, I ask that you keep an open mind. In fact, just keep it open for the duration of this book. Even if you have a familiarity with any or all the metals discussed, by keeping an open mind, you may find it easier to allow new perspectives to be presented. Then at the end we will brainstorm a handful of ideas of where to source your material, so we can start our practice of metal magic.

I believe that for us to do any type of real significant work with our metal magic practice; we need to investigate the basic foundational uses or mundane properties. This will not be an exhaustive list. As your knowledge and comfortability with metals grows, this list will grow more robust and in depth. Here in the beginning let's get a good fundamental foundation on which we can build upon. By understanding everyday uses, it will give us an excellent base on which to build on as we redirect our focus into more magical uses. Do not skip over this! It is important. Once again, you will get out of this what you are willing to put into it.

As we go forward, please understand I am not a historian, and I am using broad strokes with the dates discussed below. There may be different schools of thought as to when certain 'Ages' start and end. It is my hope that these dates will be an easy beginning guide to the concepts I wish to share. It is simplified. We are here for magical metal work, not the archaeological history of metals in all the world's cultures.

Copper

The Copper Age is thought to have started around 3500 BCE. I have even seen research that may have it earlier than that, from the ancient Native Americans in what is now the Great Lakes (3) area. Copper is a mineral that is essential to our body. Side note: (4) symptoms of copper deficiency include: fatigue and weakness, weak and brittle bones, problems with memory and learning, sensitivity to cold, difficulties walking, pale skin, premature gray hair, vision loss. By the way, nothing I state here should be taken as a diagnosis or implied as such in any way. I do not recommend adding any supplements or extreme changes in diet without consulting your medical professional. Dammit Jim! I'm a blacksmith, not a doctor! (yes, it is a bad sci-fi reference!)

I find it a nifty connection that I am able to use materials in my Work, that are also within us. How magical is that? I get a lot of enjoyment from working with copper; it has a different 'feel' than iron. It works differently in the smithy as well. It is what I refer to as a work-hardened metal. The more you work on it, the harder it gets. It can be heated (almost glowing red then quenching in water) to make it soft. Then as you work on it, it gets harder. When I say soft, I mean it gets to the point that I can bend it with just my hands. We will discuss more on how it 'feels' in a later section. Right now, I want us to focus on some of the basics.

We are surrounded by copper in our daily lives. I think it is a fairly safe bet that you have it in the walls of your living and work spaces. It makes up most of the wiring of homes and offices. It is an excellent conductor of electricity, which is why it is used for this. You may even have it for some of your plumbing. I know our house has it for our water pipes. Copper lasts a very long time, it is antimicrobial; it doesn't rust and is corrosion resistant. When it does need to be replaced, it is completely recyclable.

Copper is the first of the metal 'ages', and if you pay attention going forward, I am taking you on a little trip through them. Metal is so important they named the ages after them! My feeling is that copper is a greatly overlooked and under-used metal, especially for magical applications. But before we get to the possible magical applications, let's look at a few of the more common uses. By better understanding them, we will have a much better understanding of it in general and then we can expand and build the magical uses. You may find that there will be an expansion from general uses to your magical uses once you get everything laid out.

Copper is used in jewelry - not only due to its attractive color; it also is easy to bend and has a low melting point (around 1980 degrees Fahrenheit). Copper wire is one of the best conductors of electricity as discussed, and used in pipes, coin (the US penny was solid copper until about 1982), cookware – (it gives an even distribution of heat), roofing and gutters – (it has an incredible longevity- buildings in Europe have copper roofs that are over 100 years old, and it is lighter weight than many roofing materials), brewing kettles and stills- (It is relatively easy to mold and shape into many different forms, it conducts heat easily and efficiently, it is resistant to corrosion and it is antimicrobial). Also door handles–(easy to get different shapes, cleans up well and as mentioned before, it is antimicrobial), and much more. Copper is one of the only materials that can be recycled repeatedly without seeing any loss of performance.

Action Step - Oh No! Another List!! Give this one a little time. What around you is made of copper? Now after you have made your list, take some time and think on its uses. Close your eyes if you need to and focus on it. What kind of feelings do you get? Do you see a pattern or theme from them? Anything else, be sure to note it. This will be important later.

Bronze

Bronze is the next metal age. This age started around 3300 BCE. It's when humans really started using metals for weapons and tools. Bronze is what's called an alloy. An alloy is a mixture of at least two ingredients, in this case copper and tin. There are other additions and formulas in today's bronze depending on the grade and use of it. For our purposes, we'll keep it simple. It is more of a cast metal than forged. The two metals are melted together, then poured into casts or molds. Hence the term a cast metal. I have tried to forge it with extraordinarily little success. Not saying that it cannot be done, but I haven't had much luck with it. For me it mostly just crumbles like a two-week-old cookie when struck (like cookies last that long around here). It's likely due to the metals starting to separate upon reheating, or some such. (When I say reheating, I am referring to try to forge with it, not put it in the oven.) So, I use it mainly as an accent item. It still has a multitude of uses. It is a hard metal and does not corrode. It's used a lot in boating because of this combination of sturdiness and non-corroding. Bronze can be polished to a remarkably high shine. Perhaps you have heard of the saying, bright as bronze?

Common uses today are sculptures, hardware, doors, plaques, medallions, propellers, ship's bells, musical instrument strings, safety tools (tools where a spark could be dangerous for those that work around flammable vapors - think hammers, wrenches, pry bars and such). I'm sure I am overlooking some here.

Action Step - Yep, you guessed it. Another list. Do you know of any things around you made from Bronze? What are they? Now after you have made your list, repeat the same step that was done for copper. Invest some time and about its uses. Once again, close your eyes if you think you need to and focus on it. What comes to mind? Do you get any specific feelings? Anything else? Be sure to note it. This will be important later. Don't be discouraged if you can't think of anything. You most likely have bronze around you and aren't aware of it. It's in a lot of components that make up bigger things. If you don't have any that's noticeable, I would mark this down as an opportunity that you can possibly add. Or do some research to see if it makes up come components that you may already have. Put it on a wish list to start including it into your environment.

Brass

Although there is no 'Brass Age,' it is thought that humans started working with it somewhere around the third millennium. Today, this is a common metal used in our everyday surroundings. It is another alloy. Brass is made by melting copper and zinc together. Also, it is another metal that takes a little getting used to at the smithy for me. It does shine up rather nicely. Like bronze, it does not corrode.

Common uses today are ammunition casings (I have picked up my fair share of those), marine hardware (as mentioned earlier about not corroding, you can find it on a lot of boats and ships), musical instruments (the 'brass' section), water taps, jewelry, and although I would not refer to it as jewelry, I have polished my fair share of brass for my Army Dress uniforms back in the day. Also door handles, ornaments, household decorations (like candle holders).

Action step - Well, look at this... It's list time again! Do you know of anything in your surroundings made from brass? What are they? Now after you have made your list, repeat the earlier exercise. Take a few moments and think on its uses. Spend some time on it. What jumps out in your mind? Do you 'see' anything? Be sure to note it. This will be useful later. Once again, do not be discouraged if you don't think you have any of this around you. Brass is a very common metal and you may not be aware of it. Once again, it's also in a lot of components that make up bigger things. And again, if you don't have any that are noticeable, mark it down as something you can add to your environment.

Iron and Steel

... walking the labyrinth with the metal reinforced what I was considering. A wonderful moment to do synchronicity as I was unaware of the labyrinth beforehand. I'm not sure how to put this into words exactly as I've not considered it until now but felt there was some rapport with the iron the entire weekend. It just felt like I knew somewhat what needed to be done once shown the technique. Geoff S

The Iron Age started sometime around 1200 BCE. The words iron and steel are often interchanged; this is not technically correct though. Iron is an element that occurs naturally in the earth. Close to where I live, there were iron forges dating back to the early 1800's. This is where the iron ore is smelted (where they apply high heat to an ore, and it refines it to the base metal) to reduce it to pure iron. If you take a moment and give it some thought, iron helps sustain life on this planet. It nourishes plants and is a vital part of our very own blood. Iron Deficiency Symptoms: (5) fatigue and tiredness, shortness of breath, pale skin, brittle nails, hair loss, craving non-food substances, increased sensitivity to cold, frequent headaches, depression, and restless leg syndrome. Again, no health advice given or implied here; please consult your medical professional for that. We are connected to it; it is a part of us. On a side note, iron also falls from the sky in the form of meteorites.

The difference between iron and steel is less than 2 percent carbon. Yup, that's it. Iron plus a smidge of carbon and bingo, you got yourself some steel. Back before the Medieval period, steel was made in a bloomery. To simplify it a lot, it was a small clay chimney, about as tall as a person, with a pipe coming out of the bottom. It was filled with charcoal and then iron ore, in powder form, was sprinkled on the top. If all went well, the ore mixed with some carbon from the charcoal and at the bottom a 'bloom' of steel was formed. There would of course be more work to be done after this to get it to a useful form. A big benefit to steel over iron is that it is not nearly as brittle and it's stronger. This stuff absolutely surrounded us, steel that is. The applications and diverse types of steel will boggle your mind; it does mine. There are over 3,500 different grades of steel. For this book, I will be focusing on iron in the form of mild steel & tool steel. Once again, for sanity's sake, we will keep it simple.

We should take a breather and notice how we are surrounded by this metal nearly every moment of every day. If we observe what we do with it, we can get an understanding on which to forge our relationship (see what I did there?). Steel can become an ally if we build the right relationship with it. This includes the other metals as well.

Common uses today are reinforcing bars (rebar), roofs, internal walls, stairs, railings, bridges, in tunnels, train rail track (this makes up about half of the use of steel globally), heavy equipment, bulldozers, tractors, machinery. Approximately 2,000 pounds of steel are used to make a car. Other types of transportation like ships, trains, buses, airplanes. How about the appliances in our homes? There are washers and dryers, cook tops, cookware, utensils, microwave ovens, dishwashers, fridges, freezers, ovens, sinks, nails, hammers, scissors, axes, spears, TV's, canned goods, razors, and, and, and.... We could be at this for weeks! You get the idea by now. Whew, I may need a nap. Fun fact: the iconic American red barn "paint" is actually a compound made of skimmed milk, lime and iron oxide.

Action step - for this exercise, look around and visualize your daily life. I am going to narrow this down for you. List only twenty-five items that you know of that are made from iron or steel that you come into close contact with during the day. Feel free to add more if you think it is needed. And once again, close your eyes if you need to and focus on steel. What kind of feelings do you get? Do you get a pattern or theme from it? Anything else? Be sure to write it down.

You have made lots of lists to this point. Take a few moments and look back over them. Is there anything that attracts your attention? Do you see any overall patterns or themes? What metals have you discovered in your daily life that you hadn't thought of before? Is there anything that you find surprising?

Now that we have a marvelous list of our 'through the ages' metals, let's do some brainstorming on where we can find it.

Acquire

The easiest place and possibly quickest way to find both copper and steel to craft with for our purposes is the 'Big Box' hardware store. Although the trick to finding only the metal we need without getting distracted by all the 'shiny things' can be difficult. Copper is a common item in the plumbing section. The challenging part could be not walking out with one of everything. They also have a small selection of steel flats, bars, rods and sheets in the hardware area. It shouldn't be too difficult to find something that will be suitable for what you want. If you're undecided, sometimes smaller is better, especially when working with steel. It will humble you, quickly. For bronze and brass, you may want to search online to find it in a form that will best suit you.

You can also check out your local hardware store. I think these stores go overlooked sometimes and they very well may have just what you want without all the crowds. Not to mention the distractions. ('Oh look! I have been needing one of those!' Anyone else do this? Just me?)

And you can always order online. This is not my preferred method of getting metal, though I can't say I've never done it. I have ordered online when I need a more specialized steel in a particular size, specifically for a blacksmithing class to make tools. I personally prefer touching the metal before I buy it. As you will see in a later chapter, it can make a dramatic difference on the quality of the Work you are doing. Don't let that be an excuse from ordering online though if that's your only option. Adapt and overcome. This is your work. You do you!

Which brings us to my preferred method. It can be the most challenging and may be off the beaten path for most people. I drive for about an hour and a half to get to this marvelous epicenter of metal majesty. There is just something about a scrap yard! Sometimes they may be described as a recycling center, or your local dump may have metal access for purchase as well. Most scrap yards that I have found will let you buy and sell metal there. (Make sure they take more than just cans and such.) It will need to be what I call a sales yard; mine is a pretty large place. Keep in mind that I do this for a living, so it may not be feasible for everyone. If you get the chance though, do it. You can look at it as a quest. When I go, I usually make a day of it. You never know what you're going to find. Sometimes I go and it's like a holiday full of presents. Others, not so much. It is one of those places where I just walk around, wander and see what jumps out at me. I can pick up what someone else has trashed, and it is like I can see what 'it' wants to be. And there are also times I get something that I have no idea what I am going to use it for. Then one day, 'ah, so that is what you want to be'!

Case in point, some time ago, I had found some bronze at my local yard. It was cylindrical, an inch or so wide and probably ten inches in diameter. I did not know what I was going to do with it. As I mentioned earlier, bronze does not forge well. Needless to say, it ended up going home with me. After all these years, I have learned to listen. Metal never lies. I got it home, cut it into two pieces and flattened it out. It made two twenty-inch-long bars. They measured about ¾ inch wide and ¼ inch thick. And just recently I got that familiar 'ping.' (That is what I call the spiritual tapping on the shoulder.) I was at the smithy and boom; I saw what it wanted to be. It was mentally all finished up. I went and dug it out and measured it. Sure enough. It was the perfect length. I added some hammer texturing and shined it up nicely. Cut it to suitable sized pieces and chisel marked each one of them. They became a gift to my Beloved as an Ogham set. Twenty perfect pieces. And they are splendid- one of a kind. They feel unbelievable. Like I said, I have learned to listen. I urge that you pay attention. Metal never lies.

After you have been at this for some time, it may be the direction you want to go, going to a scrap yard. And it very well may not be. It can be challenging, exhilarating, and frustrating. You aren't guaranteed to find anything specific at any given time, so it is really hit or miss when you go. The hits though! They are fantastic! I can come home with a carload of 'junk' and be on cloud nine. 'Look at all these possibilities!!!'

Action step – Yes! And another one. Start making a tally (I did not want to use that other 'L' word) of places you could visit to see what metal you can get and where. Start with the easy ones close by. Then research other places you can go. If you can, visit several different ones. This is going to be a magical item that you will be co-creating. In my personal opinion, do not shortchange this. You may find that the big box stores are exactly what you want. Or even getting your metal online is the best way to go for you. That is perfectly ok. My thought is that by experiencing different places, you can discover the best way for you. This is one of the most important steps. All of this must work for you and you alone.

Summary of Part 1

We have covered a lot of ground. In this chapter we looked at metal "through the ages". We started at the copper age, then to the bronze age and worked our way through and up to the iron age. As a nifty bonus, brass was added in. By now you have hopefully started to see and understand how much our lives are enveloped in various metals. Very likely most have gone unnoticed until now. We have become numb to a very live world of metal that surrounds us, but together we are starting to change that, you and me. You have started to understand some of the basic properties and common uses of copper, bronze and brass, iron, and steel. It is imperative to have this understanding and awareness for us to move forward with our Work. In addition to all of this, we have also laid out and discovered places where we can find new and reclaimed metal. (I prefer the word 'reclaimed.' To me it just sounds and feels better than 'recycle'.) I also think calling it repurposed or even upcycled metal sounds good too.

Let's now turn our focus to magical metal items from Irish stories found in the Mythological and Ulster Cycles. We might just find something there that can be helpful to us as we start getting more into the feel of making our own magical tools and/or weapons from metal. I have no doubt there are numerous stories from other cultures and backgrounds; I will touch on a few of them very briefly. This is in no way a slight to any of them. I am most familiar with the Irish lore, so I'll be focusing more on what I know.

Part 2

The Rabbit Hole

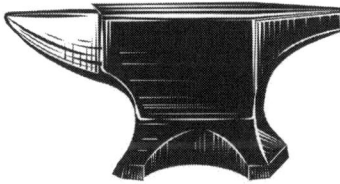

Well, here we are. This is where the start of the discovery of how far down the rabbit hole you want to go begins! Warning, this may be your point of no return. I am going to be bold and step out on a limb here. By doing all the work up to this point, you likely have a serious desire to see where this goes for you. This is a good sign and you've got a good start on your metal magic practice. It shows that you have a yearning to really add a 'next level' set of tools to your magical toolbox. Working with metals in a magical way has been life changing for me and my journey in a totally formidable way! This is not to say it has been all rainbows and unicorns. There has been painful physical, emotional, and spiritual growth involved. Sometimes growth can be unpleasant. Rewarding too.

My beliefs make my Work a reality. I have learned to work 'with' the metals. It has even become an exceptionally large part of my magical philosophy. My reality has shifted. It has made the magic of metal work for me. It has been a very tangible thing. I realize that I could be just a little bit biased, but my experience backs me up. It is my hope and desire that opening yourself to the possibilities of what metal magic can do for you, as well as with you, will help create a success of epic proportions, that it will make a huge positive difference in your life and the lives that you touch.

By all means, please feel free to adjust what I discuss to your particular tradition. I am speaking to what I have learned, what I have experienced and what I know and understand. I have no doubt that this is the way for me. I am also comfortable with the realization that what I speak to is not the only way. Like most things I have discovered in this life, there is more than one way to get the hay in the barn. The important thing is that it gets in there! So, if your tradition speaks to something different, go with it. Or maybe do some of your own research into your tradition and see what it says about metal.

I am going to lay out a few thoughts to share what got me started on this journey, and perhaps inspire you as yours begins. It was almost as if there was a trail of breadcrumbs that I was following. That and the small fact that the Goddess that I am bound to, gave me a 'polite suggestion' to do this. We will explore some of the Irish lore as it relates to metal objects and weapons that I have come across, although I am sure that I have missed some. I found a lot of them once I started looking. They seemed to be jumping out at me! It's like when you get a new car. It seems that now EVERYONE is driving the same model. Finally, after all that, we will talk about some rich and juicy possibilities going forward, as well as more opportunities to further your work.

If...,Then....

There I was. Not bothering anyone. Just minding my own business. I would like to say it was something exceptional like 'I can remember the exact moment when' or 'during a full moon, dark moon, solstice, or equinox meditation or ritual' this happened. But I can't. It was more of a series of ponderings that added up, or more like nuggets stacked on top of another. What I can say is that I am sure that most of this came about from me working at Her smithy. My smithy is dedicated to the Morrigan, hence, it's Hers. I do a lot of pondering there, at Her smithy, while I Work. Along with some contemplating, reflecting, mulling over, and sizing up, I have even been known to even decide a thing or two. I am the type of person who does some of my best analyzing when my hands are busy. It seems to free up parts of my mind that get in the way. This seems to help me seriously give things the once over.

This then, is the train of thought I went down. - *If the Gods are real*, (in my experience the Gods are very real) *then the stories about Them are also real.* Ok, no problem for me so far. Seems easy enough to digest. I mean, how would we know about the Gods if not for the stories? (I understand they are based on oral traditions that have been 'filtered' through time and cultures. I also acknowledge this is MY understanding of them.) Then this thought happened to me. *Then the stories Surrounding Them Are Also Real.* Mind = blown. (There are times it doesn't take much.) You may be thinking to yourself, well obviously. But this had just not been laid out like this in my mind. I know the Gods are real (check) and I have no issue with the stories about them being real (check). I had just not ALSO applied this same thought process to the surrounding stories. I reckon up to this point, I really hadn't needed to. Up to this point I had spent my time studying the Irish lore as it pertained to Her, the Morrigan. I had spent little to no time on anything or anyone else. When the dust settled in my mind, it was on! For me this was an important concept to digest. It really opened a whole new world for me. I started rereading bits of the lore. Searching for the metal. Remember when I mentioned that I have an animistic point of view. Re-reading the myths using this lens was a game changer for me. I started looking for the weapons, and along the way I found other items (which we'll look at in the next chapter) that took the lid off for me. This has been a pivotal point in my personal journey down the monumental rabbit hole of metal magic. And it is the basis on which I have built my practice of metal magic. To me, if the Gods exist, and the stories about them are pivotal, then the surrounding stories must also be fundamental. Giddy up!

By going back and revisiting parts of the lore and the people in them, I really started to understand how important and yet how *normal* magical metal was in their everyday lives.

Action Step - Are there any stories from your own tradition that you can circle back to and read again? Or some that you may re-evaluate? For me it is one thing to read the stories, it's a whole other ballgame to study them. What role does metal play in those stories?

Lore

Let's take a gander at some of the Irish lore (ancient Irish stories and mythology), surrounding metal magic or the magic of metal. I think you will find it interesting. Sometimes you find what you are looking for when you start *actually* looking for it:

I am going to share with you parts of a paper that set the wheels in motion for me, written by Jacqueline Borsje: Omens, Ordeals And Oracles: On Demons And Weapons In Early Irish Texts.

In this she writes,

> *The Wasting Sickness of Cúchulainn begins with a description of the fair of Samain. At this time of the year, the men of Ulster declare their victories. They bring as evidence the tongues of the men that they have killed. Some of them also bring the tongues of cattle in order to increase the amount. Each of them boasts in turn, literally 'with their swords on their thighs'. The text explains:*
>
> *… For their swords used to turn against them when they would declare a false victory. That [is] right, for demons used to speak to them from their weapons, so that their weapons were thus guarantees for them'.*

The word 'demons' here does not refer to something evil. I am understanding it as a spirit, a presence, a supernatural being. Still, I think this could be where the idea of singing swords came from. The sword itself was the guarantee of truth. Nothing wrong with boasting, telling your deeds. Note that the metal does not lie. My Grandma used to say, 'it ain't bragging if it's true'. And your sword verified your tale. I can think of more than one situation recently where a 'truth sword' would come in handy...

There are more speaking weapons to be found in early Irish literature, whether or not inspired by demons. Borsje goes on to reference a story from the Battle of Moytura, but I personally prefer reading the translation by Morgan Daimler. They translate it as:

> 'After the battle then the champion Ogma found Orna, sword of Tethra king of the Fomorians. Ogma unsheathed the sword and he cleaned it. Then the sword recounted everything it had done, because it was the way then when unsheathed [for swords] to reveal the actions they had done. Because of that legacy swords are given the tribute of cleaning them. Further, spells have been kept in swords since. And the reason demons used to speak through weapons then is that they were worshipped by people and weapons were among the sureties [116] of the time.
>
> Footnote - [116] the word here, commairge, is used to mean protection, refuge, security or of people who provide such or who acts as sureties. **It's interesting to note that it is here being applied to weapons as if they were considered people.** (bolding mine)
>
> Daimler, Morgan. Cath Maige Tuired: A Full English Translation (p. 30). Kindle Edition.'

There is a lot packed into this for me. I like this story and I always get something new from reading it each time. I have read over this multiple times before; it just did not seem to register that weapons were considered people. When this got pointed out, (I needed a sign evidently), it's like the light bulb finally came on for me.

Weapons as if they were people. Whaaaat? And spells were kept in the swords? This is where it got really interesting to me. I am going to unpack some of this as I see it. This is juicy stuff and I get excited every time I read it.

'The sword recounted everything it had done, because it was the way then when unsheathed.' So swords are not just a guarantee of what is said, they also speak the truth as well. Uh-oh, someone is always watching you. Again, metal never lies.

'Because of that, legacy swords are given the tribute of cleaning them.' I am going to address a couple of words here. The first is 'legacy.' To me legacy is a gift; it speaks to the relationship. The sword speaks of what has happened to it. And in return, it gets cleaned. The second is 'tribute'. The tribute of cleaning. A few things with this. Tribute is a show of respect or gratitude. When you are in a battle, I would imagine you would be very grateful for having a fit sword. It can also mean a payment or offering. This actually feels like an intimate relationship- the tribute of cleaning.

'Further, spells have been kept in swords since.' I think the wording on this is interesting. Not on swords, but in them. Hmm

'*And the reason demons used to speak through weapons then is that they were worshipped by people.*' As I looked at this line, it really opened up some potential in my thought process, a cause and effect if you will. One of those 'if this, then that' moments. If demons speak through weapons, then is it because they were worshipped? Worshipped. I am going to offer a few synonyms for this. Not that there is anything wrong with the word 'worshipped,' although I will admit, the word can give me the heebie-jeebies. I like to think we can expand on it and give it some deeper, lusher meaning, for instance cherished or treasured, honored, respected, or even held sacred. Isn't that better?

Finally, I want to point out something in this line. '*and weapons were among the sureties of the time.*' There are actually two points in this. The first is '*among the sureties.*' Another way to look at it is that they were an absolute certainty, a guarantee, definiteness, infallible. Unquestionable and without a doubt. What they spoke was true. **Metal never lies.** The second is what I found interesting in the footnote that Morgan Daimler added. The footnote – '*the word here, commairge, is used to mean protection, refuge, security or of people who provide such or who acts as sureties. It's interesting to note that it is here being applied to weapons as if they were considered people.*' Not a hunk of metal, but people, something literally alive and interacting. I find that interesting, don't you?

A quick note on swords. There are a lot of instances found in folklore and history about swearing on a sword. It was a very solemn act, one not taken lightly. Even Shakespeare wrote about it in several of his plays.

(There's a lot of magical stuff in Shakespeare by the way.) If you broke your oath that you swore on your sword, it was thought that the sword would turn on you or fail you and that you would find your demise. So yes, serious stuff, that.

We have now looked at a few instances where swords or weapons speak. This is one of the reasons that I asked you what you think decides the difference between a weapon and a tool. As we will see shortly, in parts of the Irish lore, it does not seem to be limited to swords. Jacqueline Borsje goes on to point this out in several of these instances:

> 'There are also weapons described in the literature that are 'alive' in a different manner. In The death of Maelodran mac Dimma Croin one can read the following about a spear: ...'*everyone who did not leave anything with it [the spear]—it would leap among them and make a slaughter of them'*.

That would be a tragic way to end your day, don't you think? A spear that moved around on its own. Note, not a sword.

> 'There is an instance in [The Intoxication of the Ulstermen], in which not just Cu Chulainn jumps, but also his weapons: ... '*his weapons jumped on/over the fore-bridge*.'

His weapons. Not just a sword. And they (more than one) followed him. Fascinating. She goes on to say:

'Another example is from [The Destruction of Da Derga's Hostel] where we find a more or less a `living' lance, called the Luin (`the Lance'), to which personifying terms are applied. When this lance is ready to shed blood, it has to be quenched regularly in a cauldron with poison; otherwise the lance will catch fire. Used in battle, this weapon is extremely dangerous. In the same text, weapons fall on the ground three times, and then make a grith, 'shout, din, uproar'. In the older translation, the weapons utter a cry, while they clatter according to the more recent translations. The Irish is ambiguous: when weapons make a noise, both din and cries can be understood by it.'

Are you starting to see a pattern here yet? Not just swords. Weapons. Alive. Moving on their own. And there is more.

The following is said about Cú Chulainn in [the Cattle Raid of Cooley]

'Then he put on his head his crested war-helmet of battle and strife and conflict. From it was uttered the shout of a hundred warriors with a long-drawn-out cry from every corner and angle of it. For there used to cry from it alike bánánaig, boccánaig, geniti glinne' and demons of the air before him and above him and around him wherever he went, prophesying the shedding of the blood of warriors and champions'

In the footnote she references a theory from Liam Breatnach that connects geniti glinne "with geined, meaning 'someone or something created/brought into being; offspring, person, creation'."

Something created and or brought into being. Curious, don't you think? Also of note, his helmet, not a sharp pointy thing.

> During the fight between Cu Chulainn and Fer Diad, the same are said to scream from the rims of their shields, from the hilts of their swords and from the butt-ends of their spears. In this example, an image is portrayed of the demonic creatures inhabiting weapons and shouting therefrom at the height of the fight.

Some more examples of weapons that are not swords, as well as weapons being inhabited. The rims of shields were often a metal band to help protect and extend the life of the shield. Hilts of swords are usually metal, and the butt end of a spear is usually metal as well. It is like an end cap to help protect the wood as well as being usable in a fight. I find it extremely provocative that in all these instances; it is metal that is the common connection. Professor Borsje sums it up well by saying:

> 'Weapons are an instrument of a supernatural power, while serving in an ordeal that testifies to the truth.' And adding: 'The instrument that is the guarantee of truth pronounces a verbal message in a supernatural way.'

This paper has had a huge effect on my Work. My personal practice of metal magic draws from some of it as well. Let's look at another example:

From the story of the Fate Of The Children Of Tuireann: (6)

> Cian then went into his own shape and said: "
> Give me mercy now." "We will not give it," said
> Brian. "Well, I have got the better of you for all
> that," said Cian; "for if it was in the shape of a
> pig you had killed me there would only be the
> blood money for a pig on me; but as it is in my
> own shape you will kill me, there never was and
> never will be any person killed for whose sake a
> heavier fine will be paid than for myself. And the
> arms I am killed with," he said, "it is they will
> tell the deed to my son."

'Even the arms with which I will be slain will recount the deed to my son.' Once again, talking metal seems to be a common thing in those times. I hear him saying in my mind, 'Come on fellas, you cannot kill me with your swords, they're going to tell on you. And y'all know this.' Story spoiler alert! They stone him to death. And no, it does not end well for those that do this dastardly deed. Go read it, it is a delightful story. And his 'son' is none other than Lugh.

In the epic Irish tale of the Cattle Raid of Cooley as translated by Thomas Kinsella in "The Tain", there is mention of *'A sword that was tempered seven times,'* which I must say is something I would have very much liked to have seen. In my mind, the material must be steel.

The Iron age started around 1200 BCE and would line up with the supposed time period of the Tain which is first century BCE to CE. I point this out to refer to the use of steel during that time vs just using iron.

Another addition to this to help explain the tempering is in Brian G Scott's 'Early Irish Ironworking' (7) he says that 'Unless carbon is alloyed with iron, the improvement of mechanical properties by heat treatments (i.e. quenching and tempering) is impossible; to temper is to heat with the specific aim of reducing hardness and brittleness induced by quenching and to balance these properties by increased flexibility.'

So there would be no need to temper the swords unless they were steel.

But wait, there's more! In The First Battle of Moytura, translated by Fraser, in section 58 it says this: *'They took up their strong, hooked shields, their venomous spears and their sharp swords with blue blades.'* Wait, blue blades? You get blue in a blade from part of the tempering process. The temperature range would be somewhere around 560-600 degrees Fahrenheit. It will make metal 'springy.' (Well, springy for metal.) This battle took place before the Tain, which means they probably were using steel then as well. Just another thing I find interesting and thought you might as well.

And one last thing. Though this is not lore specific, it does, I think, address a bit of what happened from that time to this time. Paul Budd and Timothy Taylor say it well in their book titled, 'The Faerie Smith Meets The Bronze Industry: Magic Versus Science In The Interpretation Of Prehistoric Metal-Making'

'From Wayland's Smithy to the smithy at Gretna Green where the smith performed marriages, folk custom has often associated metalmaking with magic and ritual. Yet since the Industrial Revolution a gulf has opened between material science and religion that is so wide and deep as to appear basic.'

It is my belief that this is one of the main reasons we seem to have lost touch with the magic of metal. It has become basic, common. Earlier we listed the things made of metal that are around us every day. I would think it a safe bet that some of them might have even been forgotten or gone little noticed. We have become so surrounded by it that we have now become desensitized to it. This is not a knock on anyone whatsoever; I totally get it. It's like living somewhere that has tourist attractions. You never go see them because you are close by, and they are always there and that is what tourists do. If you happen to move away, now you may want to go see them. Ask me how I know! One of my favorite places to visit now is a big attraction. And living close by, it was the last place on earth I wanted to see. How are you when you travel to some place different? Don't you want to take in the sights?

What do you say to us taking a little journey together to a place that may be a little different? Let's start with possibilities!

Possibilities

I have had my wand for a year; I am strongly attached and she is one of my best allies. She protects me and gives me strength and I adore her. The energy is the same from when I first received it. Phronesis

We have covered a wealth of information to this point. By re-examining some of the stories and lore and letting them marinate a little while, I think we can start to grasp some cool possibilities. For me, it is paramount to have some understanding of potential. If I know that it is possible, then all I have to do is figure out how to make it happen. Easy enough, right?

It brings to my mind the story of the four-minute mile. Up until 1954 they thought it impossible to run a mile in under 4 minutes. Then a guy by the name of Roger Bannister did it in 3 minutes and 59 seconds. Less than 4 minutes, right? This was a huge deal. I mean no one had ever been recorded running that fast. It was thought that it was humanly impossible to do it. It was such an enormous feat that after that, it took all of 46 days for someone to best Bannister with a time of 3 minutes and 58 seconds. Then about a year later, three more people broke the 4-minute barrier. And these three people were in the same race! Since then, well over 1500 runners have bested the time of four minutes. (Yours truly is NOT one of these runners by the way.)

The point I am trying to make is that sometimes, the very thing that is preventing us from doing something, is the limit we place on ourselves. Instead of dreaming into the world of possibilities, we just say it cannot be done. The four-minute mile is just one example of what is an exceedingly lengthy list of 'can't be done'. Can't go to the moon. Can't sail around the world. Can't fly, can't eat that whole basket of biscuits, etc. I think we should rephrase it to 'I haven't figured out how to yet.' George Bernard Shaw has a great quote. "People who say it cannot be done should not interrupt those who are doing it."

Now, am I saying that we can recreate all the stories and events in the lore, like talking swords and jumping spears? I really don't know. I am not one that has the gift to see into the future. Do I think it is possible? Sure. Why not? I mean why would I want to put limits on what can be done? Besides that, more importantly, who am I to do so? Once again, we can get all out in the weeds with the philosophy of it all. The bottom line is, I think it is possible because I see and understand the potential. I know the magic I have done with metal as well as the feedback I have gotten from others who have done so. I have no doubt what is possible. But to be honest, I am not sure how comfortable I am with spears dancing around on their own. Just cause a thing can be done, does not mean it should. But can we do the Work with metal to the point it becomes an actual magical aide? Can it become an item that has tangible energy to do Work on our behalf? I have no problem with saying most definitely! It will depend on the amount of Work one wants to invest in the practice of metal magic. I think of it as a discipline, like in any other area where you need expertise. For it to work, you must work at it. And we will talk about doing some of this Work in the next chapter.

Action Step - Take a little time and sit a spell. Take a bit of personal inventory and do some reflection. Has there been a time that you believed differently than you do now? How about as it pertains to magical possibilities? Are there things you once thought could not be possible, only to now know differently? What caused this change? How has it affected you? Do you think this is 'possible' to change in the future?

Other Traditions' Use of Metal and Magical Weapons

I am far from an expert on world traditions, but I did want to take a moment to briefly explore a few metal and weapon uses in other traditions. I think it shows that there are some stellar similarities. Let's begin with Poseidon's trident. Made by a blacksmith of course, who also happens to be the God Hephaestus. Anyway, this trident could make giant tsunami waves and flood entire islands. It could also cause earthquakes and pierce any shield or armor. Speaking of Hephaestus, He also made the Aegis, which is a shield and a weapon. It seems several different Gods had this shield at one time or another. It is also the very same shield that Perseus used against Medusa. How about Tyrfing? It is one of the magical weapons in the Norse mythology forged by dwarves who were forced to create it. So they cursed it. When it was removed from the sheath that kept it, it would kill someone. And it would also commit three foul deeds. Thor's hammer, Mjölnir anyone? In the Prose Edda, Thor used his hammer to confer blessings. It also came right back to him after he cast it.

In Hindu lore there is Vishnu's weapon Narayanastra, which has the power to launch millions of deadly missiles simultaneously. It is said to be a million times stronger than nuclear weapons. Shiva's trisulas or trident, is said to be the bane of human ignorance. It destroys physical, spiritual, and unearthly suffering.

In Chinese mythology there is the Blade of the Green Dragon. The story goes that the blacksmith was forging it as a green dragon passed by (oh to be a fly on the wall...). The dragon was killed and then forged into the blade, giving it magical powers. The Ruyi Jingu Bang is a signature item of the Chinese Monkey King. It has the power to change its size, even down to the size of a pin, multiply itself, and fight at its master's bidding. (In Chinese philosophy metal is one of the five basic elements fundamental in everything.)

The god Ninurta of Mesopotamian mythology had a mace called Sharurthat that could talk, offer strategy and transform into a winged lion. Japanese mythology talks of the sword Onimaru Kunitsuna. After having all the rust removed from it by Tokimasa (who was disturbed by nightmares due to an imp), the freshly cleansed sword then moved by itself to cut off a decorative leg of a brazier that looked like the imp of Tokimasa's dreams, freeing him from his nightly torment. I am sure there are a plethora of more examples. Please feel free to research what speaks to you. I'm simply pointing out that it seems in all cultures, around the world, in ancient times, metal was magical in one form or another. (And not all were sharp pointy things.)

Magical metal workers

Since we ourselves are about to dive into metal work, perhaps this would be a good time to look at some other famous metal workers from around the world, from the ancient times. And maybe we will get a hint or two on some personal direction. It might give an idea for study or a project or some such. Once again, I am in no way an expert on these people or their cultures, but I find it impossible not to admire some of the work.

Hephaestus. This Greek god was into all things crafty. He is the eldest son of Zeus and mostly associated with blacksmithing. To his credit belongs the trident of Poseidon and the shield Aegis I mentioned earlier. He also made the thunderbolts of Zeus, the winged helmet of Hermes, the weapons for Achilles, and more.

Brokk and Sindri. These were dwarves from the Norse tradition who where attributed to crafting Thor's hammer, Mjölnir.

Tubalcain. He is mentioned back in Genesis (a supposed descendent of Cain) and is thought to be one of the first blacksmiths of that culture.

Ptah. He is the god of craftsmen in ancient Egyptian religion.

Kothar-wa-Khasis. He was worshiped in the near east, Samaria area. He was responsible for making weapons for gods and kings as well as decorative items.

Vulcan. He was the son of Jupiter and a Roman god. He has a lot of similarities to Hephaestus.

Goibhniu. He is an Irish god of smithcraft. I say 'an' instead of 'the'. Brigid and Lugh are known for being handy with a hammer as well. Goibhniu is famous for making spears that never missed during the second battle of Moytura.

Wayland the Smith. He is an Anglo-Saxon god and blacksmith. Some think he is also a lord of the elves.

Ogun. In Nigerian and African Diaspora Traditions, he is a blacksmith and helped establish civilization.

Amakuni. He is the legendary blacksmith who played a major role in the development of the samurai swords. It is said that he became immortal from shedding his blood during the sword-making process.

One theme in these stories jumps right out to me. Many of these smiths simply supply magical tools and weapons for others to do their Work. They are not the end-user. To me that's rather interesting, and also falls in line with how I feel about the Work I do.

Summary of Part 2

I remember back in the 1980's, when I was stationed in West Germany, I was an avid reader of fantasy books. I think during that time it was a way to escape what was going on. Not a lot else to really do back then, no internet or smart phones. So, when I got back from maneuvers or patrol, I would read until I went to sleep. It was either that or play cards, and I suck at playing cards. I was intrigued with the thought of magic. Returning to the states, I was always drawn to the many stories of King Arthur. I remember thinking often, wouldn't it be neat if magic was real? You know, magic! It was not long after that I found out it was. I think my point here is, sometimes we don't know what's possible, till we know what's possible. I do not like to think in terms of impossibilities. It is not a 'can I?'; it is a 'HOW can I?'

I realize everyone will be coming into this from a different place. Y'all come from varied backgrounds and upbringing. You will have different points of view and life experiences. Some of you may have been on a pagan path for some time and others not. Some will be adept at magic and others not. And all of that is wonderful. My goal now is to get us on the same page as we go forward, which will help with embracing metal as a marvelous tool and ally. Let's embrace our experiences with an open mind and without expectations.

We have discussed some Irish lore and talked of possibilities. The importance of this section was to open our thoughts to connecting a few dots of potential, for us to start shedding some light on the mythical and magical. In the next chapter we are getting to Work; we are going to start having the metal teach us.

Part 3

F.L.O.W.

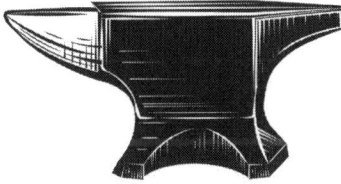

Who doesn't love a good acronym? In this section we are going to F.L.O.W. (Feel, Listen, Open and Work). This is where the rubber meets the road. All the activities done to this point have paved the way for what we will carry out next on our magical metal journey. This is what we have been working towards.

These next steps may not come easy, and that is ok. Be patient with yourself. Albert Einstein said "The world as we have created it, is a process of our thinking. It cannot be changed without changing our thinking." Try to keep in mind on 'why' you are starting down this path. I look at my practice of metal magic as co-creation. It is a lovely mix of me, the metal, and Deity. Thinking on this may be helpful to you as it gets tough or frustrating. It may very well start to be something unexplained or unusual. For either that comes up, this would be a suitable time to get that journal you have been using and start keeping track of your progress. In my practice, I have found that learning what <u>not</u> to do is as important as what <u>to</u> do. Keep good records. And keep yourself safe as you practice according to your tradition or path.

We will spend the majority of our time on the first three letters of the acronym. I believe these are the most important. I have discovered that if I take the time to set myself up for success with my Work; the process is not only easier, (depending on your definition of easy) the co-creation will become simpler. It will also be more enjoyable and will just seem to flow (see what I did there?) better. The Work will not have a forced feel to it. And I have found it to be much more powerful and impactful overall. We are going to spend time 'Feeling' our metal. Then 'Listening' to it. Being 'Open' to what we receive. This may also include ritual for you. I have included a metal meditation for those that find it useful. These steps can be challenging for some folks (raises hand). Then and only then, after these steps have been done, can deep 'Work' happen. You will get out of this what you put into it (I may have said that already, and it is worth repeating). Like with most people, the attention given and time spent with an item often leads to greater connection and understanding. I also have two examples of my own personal process from start to finish to give you some clarity and hopefully spark some ideas. Then we will discuss ritual ideas, curing, sealing and finishing off your metal.

Before we get in to the F.L.O.W. of things, I want to make two quick points:

Don't Want to Make Your Own?

There's a chance that right now you don't want to do the physical work of creating a metal item (or you just aren't in a position to do it) for whatever reason. Can metal magic still work for you? Absolutely! Can you still create an intense relationship with your metal tool/weapon without having made it? Without a doubt! You can easily apply the principles here to create and build a relationship with the metal with which you are working right now. And with that relationship, work some deep magic. You can still do most of the exercises that follow to begin your Work together. You may need to vary them slightly, adapt them to make them work for you, and that is what makes this so wonderful. There is not a one size fits all. It is you and the metal you are working with; it will tell you. It is you, building a relationship with your tool or tools. I have had people come through weekend workshops that will later ask me to co-create something for them, even though they are more than capable of doing so themselves. So just because you do not make it yourself, doesn't make it any less of a magical tool. I just want to make sure everyone understands this. It is my belief that you can become fully engaged and have a fantastic connection with the metal you are working with, whether you create the item or not. It will just be different, not less-than.

Another possibility is that you could have a tool or item that has come to you from family, a legacy item, or as a gift from someone important to you. In these cases, my suggestion would be to use these steps to build a relationship with it. If it is an heirloom or something passed down within your family, learn the story of it. Try and search out others who may have some history with it.

Repurpose, Reclaim, Upcycle

If you have followed my work for any time whatsoever, you know that most of the metal I use is repurposed. Some people might refer to it as scrap or even more eloquently, junk. I look at it like the old saying, 'one man's trash is another man's treasure.' I see it not so much as what it is, but what it can become. Now, I will admit, there is a slight possibility, it's my hesitation to throw anything away. My father-in-law would say, 'you never know when you might need that.' I have similar feelings. Growing up in southern Appalachia, we found uses for everything. We did not have much, so you got creative with what you did have. Appalachian Engineering is what I like to call it.

I do not do it to 'save money.' I live more than an hour away from my 'local' scrap yard. By the time you take in travel time and gas and treasure hunting time itself, it would be less expensive to just buy it at the local steel supplier. As I mentioned, there are times I find absolutely nothing, which is a bummer; and there are those times where I can load up my car with all the wonderful possibilities. So, it is not much of a money savings to do it that way.

I do it for other reasons, good ones, too. Primarily, I hate to waste stuff. Any stuff. To me, it is disrespectful to the world I live in to just cast something aside. Take the wood I use to make charcoal for my forge, for instance, mostly gifted 'scraps' or gathered from fallen trees. I do not waste any of it. Think about what the tree had to go through to provide that piece of wood. Try to think about all the energy that it took to make that piece of metal. The mining, refining, making, transporting, using and more. So, in a way, I refocus and redirect that energy into something else completely. I think that by doing so, it also affects the magic of it as well.

Then there is the creative side to it, looking at something and seeing the potential of it. Gee, what could you become? What do you want to be? (Now that is a good question!) I have been known to just simply grab a piece of metal and start working on it. After hammering for a time I can look at it and say, 'Oh! so that is what you want to be'. It has helped me learn to listen. Many a time I have started forging with no idea of what I needed and come out of it with something rather spectacular. I am sure She, the Morrigan, has a hand in some of it as well.

And then there are those items that just have a story to tell. What it was to what it has now become. I have made knives for people out of old hay rake tines. The kind used behind a tractor. How cool is that? That piece of metal worked in a field for no telling how long. It helped to feed someone's family. To feed the cows so someone could have milk with their cereal. To help supply the hay so someone could mulch their garden. And now it gets to have a new life as a knife for magical working or a fire striker or, or, or...

To me, my Work is so much more than just hammering out doodads. There's work behind the Work. I take pride in knowing the story of a thing. In a real way, as I co-create something, it also has a part of me as well. So yes, I could very well ditty bop on down to the local steel supplier and get some freshly made metal. All spiffy with not a speck of rust anywhere on it. Neatly stacked by size and steel type, (yes, there is a boatload of steel types as mentioned before. Think of the crayons in the great big box), still having that new steel smell. But... By saying all this, I hope what follows will make better sense.

Relationship

---

*After spending time with the metal, meditating,
and walking the Labyrinth, everything changed. I
opened myself up to the metal, what it felt like, how
it resonated with me, and then I opened myself up
to the earth and the magic around me and connected
to it. Sage W*

One morning My Beloved and I were having our
normal conversation over coffee, and the topic turned
to one I had been rolling around in my thoughts. How
to magically work with metal. It seems like it should be
a simple concept. Fairly straight forward. 'Get X metal,
do Y to it and tada! You get Z.' The fly in the ointment
is that everyone is coming from a different direction,
background, thought process, history, etc. You get
the idea. Listen. For me, I know I learn so much more
from listening than talking. Give it a day or two. Wait,
what? A day or two? This does take some time. And
Yes, it is worth it. Be patient with yourself. This may
be something very new to you. It will take some time.
Don't cheat yourself and try to cut corners.

Let me take a moment and expand on what I mean
by 'Work'. I am using it as both a verb and a noun.
Merriam-Webster's Unabridged Dictionary has verb - 1C:
*to exert oneself physically or mentally, especially in sustained
effort for a purpose or under compulsion or necessity* and the

noun - *1C: sustained physical or mental effort to overcome obstacles and achieve an objective or result.*

Where am I going with this? 'Work' is different from a quick fix, a google search or picking up a doodad from the store or online shop? I also realize that I am much different now than I was 30 years ago when I started down this path. And my oh my, how different things are. I cannot imagine how overwhelming it could be for those starting out now. I can search for anything online and get an answer. Is it THE answer? You know, the answer I need, for me? And how does one really know? My answer: Relationship.

Relationship: *a state of affairs existing between those having relations or dealings* (back to good ole Merriam-Webster's Unabridged Dictionary)

I don't think this applies to just metal magic; I think it can also apply to many areas of magic and of life. Everything is connected. For me, to really understand and feel comfortable working with something, I must get to know it. Try to understand it. Dare I say, have a relationship with it. Yeah, I am a bit of an animist. I am "comfy" working around things that are known to me.

How do you build a relationship with metal? This is the million-dollar question. And that is precisely what we are going to address.

Feel

...the minute I held it in my hand I could feel its power of protection as well as its magic! Arlene B

Have you ever walked into a place, and it gave you the heebie-jeebies? As soon as you crossed the threshold, you could not wait to be someplace else. Almost any place else. Likewise, how about a place that was comfortable and inviting. That feeling of you being surrounded by a warm hug. I have found metal to be remarkably like both of these situations. It is the energy or vibration it gives off, the spirit of it. If there is a chance you are using repurposed metal, this vibration is especially noticeable. Being able to discern the feel of your metal will be a big determination on your next steps with it. Not to say it's for certain what your item will or will not be, just a key step in understanding it, as well as how you may want to approach it. Think of the metal as being 'a person' and that this is your introduction to each other. How would you go about doing that? Look at it as if y'all are going on a first date.

Action step - If you have not already done so, now would be a good time to gather some metal. Try to find a piece of each type (copper, bronze, brass, and steel) if you can, to see if there is a difference to you. And if so, what difference. For now, I want you to focus on what you "feel". How do the various metals feel different to you? What are your very first impressions? Are they warm or cold? How so? What comes to mind? Experiment. Catalog it. Do not rush this! You can also do this with metal tools and items you already have. What feelings do you get from them? Even if you do not want to get into making your own items, I would still highly encourage you to get bits of the different metals. This way you can have a first-hand feel of the differences in their energy. I would highly recommend that you take your time with this. Enjoy the process. Explore. Experiment. Feel free to refer to earlier mentioning of metals in chapter 1 for a refresher. A nifty exercise for you to try would be to hide the metals from your eyes and see if you can tell which is which just by the 'feel' of them.

*I am now going to share with you my general feelings of each metal from my experience with working with them. These are not etched in stone. You may have a completely different response, sensation or even experience. And that is ok. Whatever impression you get, spend a little time trying to understand it. It will give you deeper insight on the future uses for you. And how it can be helpful in your Work.

For me **copper** is warm and fluidic. Healing and comforting. There is an elegance to it, not in a soft way. Majestic. There is a type of gentle wisdom. It has an ancient feel to me. It is also a fantastic conductor of energy.

Bronze is strong and unyielding. Dazzling and intense, like it is lit up from within. Reflective and magnifying. Radiating. There is also a distant feel to it. It has a regal energy to me.

Brass has that comfortable energy to it. Enduring and rugged. Sleek. Utilitarian. It feels like it has a natural belonging, like it morphs to fit into its surroundings.

Steel is protective. Cold, but not in a necessarily unfeeling way. Laser-like focus. Powerful and stout. Resolute and dependable. There is a nobility to it. Loyal and enduring. An inner deep strength of the ages. Confident. Grounding. There is also a connection to the heavens- it falls from the sky. As above, so below. I also feel a great strength with steel.

Action Step: What similarities or differences did these descriptions have with what you felt, when you held the different metals in your hand? With this in mind, start thinking about how you could use each metal in your spiritual practice. What purposes could they serve?

Take a look at some of my Work, and it should not be very hard to spot my feelings for each metal from the end results. What I forge will mostly line up with these, although there are always exceptions. It is metal, and as you will learn, it has a mind of its own.

Listen

Once I started to do the things I had never done (chopping wood and building the fire) I felt more connection to the land, which led me to feel the design process more intently, which had me listening to the metal in a different way to what I normally would do. Coral M

I remember when all this (waves arms to include the area around Her Smithy), started. I am not sure if I have mentioned it yet, but I can be a bit slow at times. Some may say hard-headed. I was trying to make something (although I can't for the life of me remember what). I grabbed a length of metal and started to work. It did not go well. Like mangled badly not going well. I do remember it was something I had made many times before because I was thinking, 'huh, this piece of metal must have gotten past quality control there.' So, I grabbed another and went to work. Nada. Another mangled mess. (I actually think that piece of metal may have ended up flung into the woods all mysterious like…). I remember sitting down, taking a deep breath, and asking, 'what am I doing wrong?' What came back was, 'have you tried asking?' And my reply was, 'I thought that is what I was doing?' See, hard-headed…. But all joking aside, I wasn't asking. And I wasn't listening.

The most important part of working with your metal is listening. This step is where your patience may need to kick in. If you are one of those folks that don't have much patience, guess what? The metal with fix you right up. Some can hear the metal right away and others, not so much. No judgment- there are people who have a natural affinity for metal magic, and others who must learn it. I had to learn it. Rather I should say, it was taught to me. I will explain more about this in a minute. There are a few ways to accomplish effective listening I have found. It will depend on the size of your metal; for now, let's keep it to a size that can be easily carried by you. The two methods that have been most effective with listening are sitting with and walking with your metal. Your metal may have diverse layers to it; by that I mean the story or stories of it. (Your metal may have several stories). I have found this most often the case when I am working with reclaimed metal. It will also depend on what your metal 'wants' to be. And you can learn this too. That is what this step is all about. Communication. Think of this as a form of co-creation. You and the metal.

I have a couple of ways in which to work with the metal I want to use. I will most often seek metal that wants to be what I need to make. I have a firm idea of what I want to do and listen around till I get that 'pick me' ping. I will walk around the smithy, running my hand over different sections of metal or rummaging through buckets until I get to the one that just 'feels' right. And there are times I just make what the metal wants to become. That is simply picking a piece, listening for a while, and starting the forging process. No agenda. Next thing you know, boom, there it is. Those times are wonderful, and it happens more often than you think. I have seen it often in my weekend immersions I have here. I believe anyone can do it. You will have to work at it yes, but it's doable.

Back to you. Both sitting and walking with your metal work best in nature in my experience. Get outside if you can. If not, no worries. Simply find yourself a quiet space. Where you won't be disturbed. First just sit with it. Think of meditating and focus on the metal. Take time to be alone with your metal & tune in to it. Reach out to it. Listen.

The other process which I find very effective is walking with it. On our land we have a labyrinth built into the woods. I will take what I need to work on or with and go there, walk, and listen to it. For me, at times there is something about the movement that gets the juices flowing so to speak. Many of my weekend class participants also mention that this was a game changer for them. I know not everyone is going to have access to a labyrinth, but a hike or nice walk in the woods could also be very effective. On a small side note, I have also found that when I am doing sigil-creation for metal, I can walk around a bit with the metal, then sit down and just scribble until the right symbols show up. So 'listening' with my pen and paper, so to speak. It takes some practice. You will know when it's right for you. If you are unsure, meditate on it some more. Give it a day or so or even a moon cycle. When it is right, you will know. It is like the feeling of finding the right puzzle piece that fits.

Try both of these to see which may be most comfortable for you. Use the same metal for both and see if there is a difference.

Action Step - Journal time! What did you learn? What did you 'hear'? Were there any sensations that showed up? Did you see anything? What was the metal like? Cold? Warm? Did you feel a vibration or energy? Write everything down about the experience.

Open

When I wear the hair sticks, I can definitely feel them adding to my own protections, but I feel an innate strength radiating from them and into me. It's as though they are a direct communication line to my goddess and I even feel a closeness to her when I wear them. Michelle F

Be open to the messages you are getting (or NOT getting) from your metal. I think this can be a tricky step. Anyway, while this step is often overlooked, it will determine the power of your Work. As I mentioned in an earlier step, in the beginning I often decided what I wanted to make without consulting the metal I was using. Not that what I wanted to make was wrong, it just didn't always fit the metal I was using. Be open to trying new things. If you do not change, things won't change for you. It reminds me of the saying about insanity. "The definition of insanity is doing the same thing over and over again and expecting a different result." (By the way, the quote seems to have originated in one of the twelve-step communities, not Einstein as some believe.) I often hear others say, 'this is the way I normally do this' or 'I've always done it this way'. My first thought is, 'and how is that working out for you?'

I teach things a certain way because I have found that it works. I have already done the trial and many error exploration. I am not saying this is the only way, just a way that I know; I teach it this way because it works for others too. It very well may not work for you; there is an easy way to find out... if your goal is to make a magical item with the metal you have, getting it to agree and be all for it is an extremely good idea. I look at it several different ways. You can go on about your business and try to force your will on it. You know, be a bully about it. Decide that you know best. Personally, I wouldn't recommend this route. Ask me how I know. You can go through the above steps and if the metal you have is all about it, there you go. It cannot wait for you to start. Forge on! But if you aren't *feeling* or *hearing* agreement, circle back and find a piece that wants to be what you want to make. What you have may not want to be what you are trying to create. And that is ok. It happens. It wants to be something else. Trust it. The metal never lies. Just my opinion of course. I have found that when I do set it aside and come back to it later and make what it wants to be, it is most satisfactory for both of us. The work is easier, cleaner, stronger.

Something to keep in mind, if you have a length of metal and you are only using a bit of it, the other things that you make from it will be connected. It is the same metal. This is important! And immensely magical. For instance, if I am making a pendant for protection, it is very possible the rest of the metal that is left quite possibly will also have that same type of intention and energy. It will all be connected. Cool huh?

Getting a 'no' from your metal doesn't always mean never. It could very well simply mean 'not right now'. Be open to change. Be open to a different direction. Be open to 'keep on keeping on'. Be open to waiting (yeah, I don't like this one either). Be curious. Be flexible. This is your magical tool, item, or weapon. There may be something else it wants to be. It might need to have something else with it. I would think that you would very much want it to be an ally with you. Please take into consideration that you are a co-creator in this work. It is a partnership. What type of partner do you want to be? I am not trying to overly harp on this. I just want to hammer home how crucial this can be. I have done it. Others have done it. I am trying my best to keep you from a 'teachable moment'. Take a couple extra moments and be in right relationship. Even if everything is hunky dory, be open to adapting. You could very well get a 'yes *and*' sense. 'Yes, you could do that. And you could also do...'

Action Step – Ponder these questions: Have you ever tried to make something, and it just would not work? No matter how hard you tried. Then changed something- even if it is a small thing- and Bingo, you are off and running? Maybe even had to set it aside and come back to it later. Have you ever been in that 'space,' that space where it seems that time is of no matter? Everything just is right. It is like you are 'plugged in' to something greater than yourself. For me, it can feel like being an active spectator. And have you ever had something planned out and then boom, something completely different happens? How did it turn out? Better or worse than you thought? If you already have your tool or item, you can use this step to see if there are other ways to use it. Or even how you can better work with it. Write your thoughts in your journal.

Metal Meditation

I offer this short meditation as a different way for you to get in touch with your metal. It is something that I have had success with. Feel free to use it as is or change it to best fit your needs. The important thing is that you find a way to get in touch with your metal. To Feel, Listen and be Open.

Get comfortable. Just breathe, relax, let go for a moment. Breathe. – Let go of the tension of the day. Give yourself permission to just be here for a time. - Move your focus to your breathing, in and out. In and out. Focus on the In - and then out of the breath. Relax. Take 3 deep breaths. Breathe in and hold it. Breathe out. Breathe in and hold it. Breathe out. Last time, breathe in and hold it. Breathe out. Return to normal breathing. Relax. Let go.

You find yourself walking in the woods, an item of metal in your hand. – As you are walking along, you notice that there is a tall tree canopy, very little underbrush. - The light is dappled as it is cast on the forest floor. - You hear dried leaves crunch beneath you as you walk. - You are walking along a path that seems to be an animal trail. You can you smell the richness of the earth - The walk is easy and gradually slopes downhill. - You feel a slight breeze against your face. - The trail continues downward - and you notice that it is leading you towards a small foot bridge. – As you reach the bridge, you see and hear a gentle creek that runs beneath it.

You use the bridge to cross the creek. As you reach the other side, you walk between two large trees that the trail leads through. - As you proceed between them, it feels like you have walked through a bubble of protective energy. – You stop and take a deep breath in and out. – You feel safe, secure, protected.

You see that the path leads on, and you keep to it as it leads you around a bend. The path parallels the creek. You start to notice the smell of a campfire. The woods open into a small clearing by the creek. You see a small fire in a pit surrounded by stones. A wooden bench is set up for you by the fire pit. Have a seat and hold your metal item in your hands.

What sensations do you notice?

Does it have a temperature?

Does it have a vibration?

Do you notice any emotion or feeling?

Are you able to see any markings or colors on the metal?

Does it have anything to say?

Is there a story it wants to share?

Does it have any requests?

Does it want you to do something with it? Or not do?

After you feel you have gotten your answers, give thanks to your metal. Give thanks to the fire and this place. Know you are welcome here and can return anytime.

Walk back over to the path you came in on and retrace your steps out. Enjoy your stroll back as you hear the creek. Cross back over the bridge. As you make your way back up the gentle incline you start returning back to your body. Wiggle your fingers and toes. Slowly open your eyes and give it a good stretch. Write down your experience while it is fresh in your mind.

Work

---

*I have a lot more respect for metals since the course.
Copper feels friendlier, and iron feels even deeper
and more dense. The tools that I made remain
available to me, and I know the time will come when
they are exactly what I need. Mara*

This is where it can all come together. In the Projects section, we will talk in detail about four projects that you should be able to do with minimal tools and skill level. Remember! Have fun with it. It will be your Work! Practice is what it takes for it to work. It IS a practice. Be patient! You may even decide (I might even recommend) that the first item you make is a 'practice' piece. That way you can get used to the tools and get the system down that works for you. By doing this, it can also relieve some pressure of getting it 'right' the first time and learn what not to do. I get a lot out of learning what not to do. Have I mentioned that yet?

For those that have a metal tool or item that you work with already, this is a time where you can offer up some additions to it. Does it need some sort of enhancement? I have known folks who simply take an engraver or permanent marker to enhance their metal altar plate or candle dish (with a protective sigil or other design for example). Does something you have need a little wire wrapping or an added metal charm? This too can be part of your metal magic. Allow yourself to be creative. What does 'it' want? You can always circle back and start again with the first step of Feel and work through them again to see if anything changes. For me, sometimes it's easy to 'shut down' when I do not think I can do something. When I get a different perspective and some options that make it more feasible, it opens up a brand-new world. I have learned (She is still teaching me), to stop putting limits on myself by what I think I cannot do. I try to focus on solutions. A 'no' becomes a 'not now.' Instead of 'I can't,' I try to think of 'how can I'. That usually requires me to do something differently or to add something into what I am currently doing. Or even to look differently at what I am trying to do. Focusing on being a 'problem solver' has so much more power in it than allowing situations to stop you. I can't count the times I have gone into a project and have absolutely no idea how it was going to turn out, or how I was going to get it to work, but trusting the FLOW of it. And to be honest, it usually turns out better than what I had originally pictured in my mind. And there are other times that I learned what not to do. Learning what not to do is an unbelievably valuable thing for me. It will save me time later. I may not know what to do, but I will surely know what not to do. As I said before, have some fun with it!

I would like to add one more thing if you will allow me to ramble a bit more. Students often ask, 'how did you make this thing?' I will usually explain how I did it. Then I will say, 'would you like to know what I would do differently next time?' That is a valuable question, don't you think? 'If you had to do this again, how would you do it?' It changes the conversation to more of an experiential one with some nuggets of wisdom along the way. Just a thought.

I also want to mention another vital ingredient-Time. You must invest it to have a strong and powerful relationship to your Work. There is no substitute. No shortcuts. No work around. I have heard 'I don't have that much time', 'I can only spend a few minutes a day', 'I forget what I am doing'. You won't have a deep relationship with your Work if it is an afterthought. It must be a priority for you. You will get out of this practice what you put into it. If it is important, you'll find a way.

Use What You Have

Please don't be intimidated if you are in a position that will prevent you from hand-making or enhancing your own metal items. Not everyone can or even wants to. You can still create some powerful items by simply connecting with the metal that you already have. You can use the F.L.O.W. process for any of your current magical metal tools or items. Build a relationship. Make sure you write down your experiences. This will help you as you continue to work your practice.

The Blade or That's What She Said

I want to share the process of making of what I humbly refer to as 'The Blade'. I think this may give you an idea of how this may go from start to finish. Each time I make a magical item, it is always different. The item is different, for different needs, different people, different metal. What is the same is the way I go about it. Over the years I have made several knives, athames, daggers, spear tips and the like, mostly for others to do their Work. I do have a simple knife that I made years ago for personal use. Nothing fancy, more utilitarian. Honestly, I never had the desire or felt the need to make one. Until recently. See if you can spot the steps.

As it happens from time to time, I got that 'ping'. Those that know me well, know I refer to it as a 'polite suggestion.' Anyway, what I got was, 'I want a blade.' My first reaction was, 'no ya don't'. I didn't say it was a smart reaction, it was just the first one I had. Ok then, 'what kind of blade do you want?' Crickets. So, I started rummaging through selections of metal. I start with feeling some new shiny tool steel that I have. I mean, it is for Her right? Nope, not it. I wander over to a bucket that has an assortment of 'junk' metal. In it were several old rusty files, lawn mower blades, bush hog blades, horse bridle bits, old tiller tines and other miscellaneous metal. 'This!' is what I felt as I handled one of the tines.

A little side story about the tiller tines (I like stories). When we purchased our home, it had been abandoned for at least a year before we moved in. And this place was not well taken care of before then. There were two 'dump' sites on this property, (not legal ones mind you). We have been cleaning them up little by little as we go. I refer to them as my personal hardware store. If I need something, I just go plunder through them and I will usually find an item that will work. One of the days that I was pulling out trash to take to the landfill, I ran across theses tiller blades still attached to the shaft. No tiller in sight. I did what I always do, I set them aside. You never know when you might need those. As it just so happens, I did, years later.

Back to the current story. I picked it up and looked at it. I have made bearded axes out of these, but never a 'blade'. This is going to have some size to it. Now before I forget, it was also 'suggested' that I have this done before the Morrigan's Call Retreat (MCR), an annual event held in CT in June. At the time, I had no idea why it needed to be done by then. I mean, I wasn't planning to sell it. Still not sure exactly why to this day, although I do have my suspicions, as you'll see. So off to Work I go. 'A blade huh?' as I get a good feel of it. Passing it from hand to hand and flipping it around. Still all rusty and dirty. Interesting, I thought. Morrigan, daughter of Ernmas, the 'she farmer.' Tiller tine, I can dig it!

I spent a few days with the tine. Thinking of the stories it had. How was the work that it did to the land that helped feed someone's family? How many years? Was it excited about its next adventure? This is the start of our relationship. Me and the Blade. It is important to me that I get to know the metal I am working with. It is important that it, the metal, wants to be what I need it to be. To give you a general timeline of this process, I started around the first of May.

On about the 5th of May, I start working on the blade shape. I set my space and container, start the forge, and go to Work. Simply focusing on what it wants to look like and become. At this point in the endeavor, I am just an active spectator. Within mere hours the blade takes shape. I am surprised at the speed and ease this happens, yet not surprised. If that makes sense.

I now have a rough forged blade. Now what? I know! I have this beautiful black walnut that I can use for the handles. Then I hear, 'No, metal'. Wait, what? Metal! Ok, um, Houston, we have a problem. I had planned on using copper for the hand guard (the wider piece that separates the handle from the blade). But handles are supposed to be wood. Or so I thought.

Another side story. It goes back to when I made a primitive cottage dedicated to Her. I created a plaque for it made of steel, copper and bronze. It felt 'Through the Ages'. The copper age, the bronze age, and the iron age (steel is iron with 2% or less carbon. This is the simplified version). She has been here, through the ages. I now have a series of pendants that I make for those that are dedicated to Her. The collection is called, literally, "Through the Ages." Each one is unique to the wearer and yet all are made of copper, bronze and iron (steel). I say this to give you some sort of feel of what was transpiring in my head as I went through this process of figuring out my next steps.

I have a copper hand guard. The next logical step is to make the handle out of bronze. All three metals.

Problem solved. I admit, I was really feeling good about going with the bronze for the handles. But 'Nope'. Not great. You see, I can't forge bronze. Bronze is a cast metal. I think it is better for me to say I haven't figured out a way to forge with it yet. I use it for accents to special items. The bronze I have is not wide enough to fit the shape of the handle. I had to hammer out sections to widen it. I had to be easy with it. Too much and it will crack and split. It is tough metal. It just doesn't take kindly to making it change shape. One side done! That wasn't so bad. This is moving right along. Started working on the other side. You can probably guess what happens next. Crack!

Now what? At this point I'm thinking that I should have just stayed with the black walnut. I'd be done by now and it would be lovely. 'No! METAL!'

I have now found myself in a bit of a pickle. I have a copper handguard and half a handle of bronze. The rest of the bronze I have won't work for the other side, it's the wrong thickness, way too thin. It is in times like this, I find it best to listen. Really listen. I grabbed the blade and down to the Cottage I went. I find it easier for me to listen sometimes when I am down there. Everything becomes less complicated. I think being in nature is always a big plus when it comes to sorting out something. And sure enough, there it was. Copper. I had been so hung up on the hand guard being copper that I wasn't open to the idea of copper ALSO being on the handle as well. The trick now would be to find some that matched the size and shape of the bronze side. Spoiler Alert! I found it. An easy, perfect match.

Extraordinarily little work needed to be done to get it to fit right on there.

The bronze I have been mentioning is the very same bronze piece that I made my Beloved's Ogham set out of. Nifty huh? What's even more nifty is that the copper piece I used for the other side of the handle is what I used to make my own Ogham set. If that ain't some next level magic afoot-ness, I don't know what is!

Everything was humming right along now. When I started out on this journey, I had a name for this blade firmly in mind. It was *Ecin*. Which in Irish translates to *Indeed* if I am not mistaken. I figured this was a grand name. Has the Morrigan vibe all over it. Well, as things happen, that is not the name *it* chose. It decided on another name, *Afraigid!* Which has now been chiseled into the copper side of the handle. This word is from Her incitement poem found in Cath Maige Tuired [the Second Battle of Moytura]. It translates roughly to *Arise!* This obviously also has a very Morrigan vibe to it. So there!

Another thing that might make you go hmmm. As I was finishing it all up, I was thinking, this thing is going to be all wonky. All that metal is going to make it all off balance and uncomfortable to hold. Oh nay nay! It's perfect. I could not have planned it better.

As I mentioned earlier, I started this undertaking around the first of May. I finished assembling The Blade around the 18th. It took me several weeks to complete. And was done in time to get to know it for a week or so before taking it to the MCR. It was not dedicated before leaving to attend; I had not even made a sheath for it yet. I simply wrapped it up in a big section of leather.

I am not going into a lot of detail as to the adventures of the blade while at the MCR. I feel most of those things are private and should remain so. I will say it had the honor of not only bearing witness to a handfasting, it also was a part of guarding the temple in the evening. There was a significant reason for it to be there. Not just to be in attendance, but to be in action, in service. Doing its Work. It now has new stories. And I believe this is just the beginning!

Did you notice anything? Could you pick out the FLOW?

Weekend Workshops

How to even describe the experience of doing Ravens Keep Forges magical blacksmithing class. I can give words, but nothing will be adequate to sum up the experience. From start to finish it is one of the most powerful things you'll ever do. Allen B

Participants are able to camp on our land during my weekend workshops, allowing them to disconnect from the outside world. Living in the country does have its benefits. Where we are, there is little cell phone service if any. It really allows an in-depth focus on the FLOW. It is amazing to experience and witness the change from beginning to end. Not just in the understanding, but in Co-Creation as well.

These are really something. To me, it is a weekend that seems longer and then again, flies by more quickly than merely a few days. I find it extremely challenging to put into words what the weekend is about. One thing I have noticed about the metal magic weekends is that they differ from any of the others I host; it seems everyone goes through some sort of initiation here, of varying degrees and challenges. I will explain none of them here, not my place to. It is a big part of magically working with metal. And not with 'just' the metal. Seeing it as part of a whole.

It's also interesting to see what people are initially wanting to make, and then what they actually craft.

Putting oneself in a position to go with the F.L.O.W. can be tough. And what they leave with is spectacular. I have been at this a long time, so I can tell the difference between what is merely shaped and what is co-created. And full disclosure, the land helps with this. It is a part of the journey and I believe creation.

To see the glow surrounding everyone on Sunday is something to behold. It is a difficult weekend. Everyone works hard. Everyone must overcome something. Over the weekend, most will do things they never have before, in a way they've never done. New ideas are discussed, and space is given to explore.

No matter how someone comes to this weekend workshop, they are different when they leave. The feedback I get is that what transpires in the three days is greater than the imagination. It was so much more than their expectations. And I address this from the beginning. In our orientation, I ask that everyone release your expectations and let the weekend come to you. This is also part of the challenging work. To give yourself permission to just *be* for a few days, without expectations. Let the 'magic' happen. The metal never lies. I bring this up to give you an idea of how impactful metal magic can be. It is something. And it is different. I do not think any two people have the exact same experience.

Summary of Part 3

Sam made me two versions of Fionn's Window, one with forfeda and one without. I could feel the energy of both of them immediately and I could feel the difference between them. I could tell which one was used for bindings and closings and which one was not right way. Izzy S

We've covered a lot in this chapter. Some concepts may be new to you, some may not. My goal was to get you to be in alignment with whatever type metal you may be working with. To think in a different way about metal magic. To go with the F. L.O.W. and let the metal work with you, to be a partner, a co-creator. I have found this to not only be easier overall, but it has also made my work so much more powerful. It is my belief that if I am in tune with how the metal feels; I listen to the message it has for me, what it may want, and be open to changes, my work will be in tune with what needs to occur. Or, in some cases, I may even need to use a different piece altogether for what I am making. I strongly encourage you to take the time to build a relationship with the metal that you are building a practice with. Think of it as more than simply a tool.

I gave you a meditation to use to get in touch with your metal, as well as an example of what the process can be like from start to finish.

Next, let's look at tools needed and some that simply will be nice to have. Yea tools and stuff!!! Then we'll discuss some projects that you can do to create your own, as well as ritual ideas to enhance the magic.

Part 4

Tools, Projects & Rituals

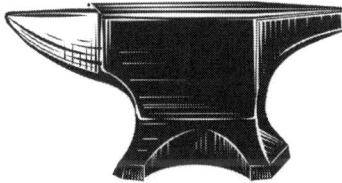

One of the guiding principles that I have, is to try to be as cost effective as possible. See if I can find something that will make it work. Humans have been working metal for an exceptionally long time without fancy equipment. The last thing I need to do is collect more stuff- I have plenty. I highly encourage you to start where you are and add as you go along. Even tough it out for a while or try to figure out how you can get it done with your current situation. That is also part of the Work as well. The 'hard' is what makes it great at times. I am going to try to keep this to what you may have on hand, or at least not break the bank at a discount tool store or online.

My goal is getting you to do the work without getting bogged down with what you do not have. Let's figure out how to make it work, so you can spend time co-creating, not collecting. Although, who doesn't like a shiny new tool? I am approaching this with the thought that many of you may live in an urban area. If you live at a place or know where you can dig a hole for a forge, then it could change how you work with this. I know all that follows here may not work for everyone, depending on your situation. It should at least give you a few ideas on how you can make it work for you. My goal is not to get you into blacksmithing. It is to get you into metal magic. Be creative! The following tools and exercises I have compiled will give you a good start into creating your own. If you feel that other tools or items will work better for you, then you do you. There is more than one way to do things much of the time. And what I am offering is only one of those ways.

As a reminder, you do not need to *create* your own magical metal tools for them to be powerful. Just because you do not make your own items, I think it in no way makes your Work 'less than'. I still would like for you to review the tool list in case you want to alter or enhance something you already have or acquire.

Action Step- You need to find out where you are in the tool department. Be thinking of what you currently have on hand. Make that list! This will help with what you need to add, if anything.

I am going to start out with what I think is a minimum or 'got to have' tools. Then we will look at several worthy upgrades, meaning tools that would be nice to have. Then finally, 'splurge-able' tools.

"Got to Have" Tools

To complete the projects I have suggested, these are tools that I think at a minimum, you will need. You may already have many of these, but if not, they will be inexpensive to get. As mentioned before, my focus will be trying to see how low we can go. I believe this will help you in focusing on the Work. I'd rather have you spending time with your metal, then spending time and money shopping. Although, tool shopping......

Bare Minimum Tools:

Ball Pein Hammer. Not a carpenter's hammer. Many may call a carpenter's hammer a claw hammer. Do not use that, please. It is not designed for this type of work, and it can end up being dangerous. Just don't. So, get you at least a ball pein. These are the hammers that have a flat face on one side and what looks like a ball on the other. In fact, get two of them in different weights if you can. I would get one that is 16oz and one that is 24oz or 32oz. If you can only get one, I would go with the lighter; I use a 16oz often. You may even find them in a set with many sizes, which would allow you to experiment with different ones. It is more about hammer control than it is about seeing how much smashing you can do. The ball end can add a nifty texture to your work. Think hammered copper. So, one tool, two uses. A twofer!

Tape Measure. Six feet should be more than enough. If you have one that measures more than that, no worries. You may even be able to get by with a large ruler.

Quench Tank. This is a water-filled vessel used to quickly cool your metal. In the classes I teach, I use a large metal coffee can. Empty of coffee of course and filled ¾ with water. I have seen others use plastic. For me, the metal one is much safer. A five-gallon bucket filled at least half-way with water may do the trick. Just be sure not to touch the plastic sides with your metal! Hot metal and plastic do not mix.

Hack Saw. You will need this to cut your metal. Yes, it will be work. And yes, you can do it! A hacksaw is a great friend. And while you are at it, get some extra blades. They are not awfully expensive, and you can go through them quickly. It is a consumable item. There is not a big difference to me in the quality of the blades. I still go through them at the same rate regardless of cost.

File For Metal. Once again, you may find these in a pack of 3 or more in different shapes. If you can only pick one, get a flat file. If you can get a half-round file, do so. I am not referring to what's called rasps or needle files; however, some sets may include all these. Once again, an area for you to experiment with and learn if you do get a set of them. This will help with any rough edges you may have.

Sandpaper. I have seen packs of various grits at dollar stores. You really do not need anything fancy. This would be for taking off some scale, smoothing and polishing up. It would be nice if you could get a choice of different grits so you can see what works best for you in the different stages of your projects. An assortment pack starting around 60 to 80 going up to around 220 to 400 grit should get you going good. The bigger the number, the finer the grit. A little elbow grease will also be needed with this.

Chisels. You will be using these for marking your metal. Do not get wood chisels please! I know you can get what are called 'cold chisels' inexpensively. They are made to work on cold steel. There should be a set of them. If you can get a few **punches** in your set, that would be a nice bonus. You will want those punches if you continue with this. You can use chisels and punches to lay out marks on your metal. As you spend time with your design thoughts, thinking of straight lines and dots will be helpful. (Curves can be a challenge.)

Pliers. This is where things can get a little tricky. Every type is different. The two I would suggest would be **slip joint** and **needle nose**. Nothing at all wrong with channel locks, vice grips, and others. If you have them, they will work. I am just trying to be budget friendly here. You may be able to get these in a set as well. I find 8-10 inches is a good size.

Vise. Specifically, a tabletop or clamp-on type. They should be around two to two and a half inches. It will be used for holding your material as you cut it and other processes you may need. If you are in an area where you can or do have a workshop area, a larger vise (4-inch size or larger) would be nice because it would also have a bit of an anvil or striking surface with it. It will be useful down the road, but not a must-have. The inches address the jaw size in case you were wondering. Not having this item will not be a deal breaker, but it can make life much easier as you learn.

Marking Pencil. You may get away with using a regular #2 type pencil. I personally cannot see the markings of those very well. What has worked well for me is a grease pencil (I use this mostly for marking to cut metal), or permanent marker. (It will not be permanent in my experience. They can be used for marking to cut and for design layout. They can be thicker for the marking and a finer tip for the designing.) A welder's pencil works well too; I have seen these in both red lead and silver. I prefer the silver because I can see it better for the marking. It is also used to draw on the metal you are working with to design and mark it out.

Torch. I use a propane torch. You can get one at the big box stores. You will need this to heat your copper to work it as well as to temper your metal if you so desire. I have heard of others using a butane torch as well. It will take a little practice to get the hang of using it. And as with all tools and equipment, make sure you follow the suggested use, directions and safety from the manufacturer.

Steel brush. I have seen these at the dollar store. They have a long wooden handle. They are helpful to clean up your metal and get some of the bigger flakes off, especially if it has a bit of rust or such on it.

Journal. I hope by now you have one well under way to being filled up. You may want to continue adding to it or you may want to have a separate one for the 'work behind the Work' if you will. Either way, take notes. What is working well for you? What are you being challenged with? Here is a question that will help you greatly – 'What would you do differently next time after you created something?' As I mentioned earlier, in my teaching I always follow up an explanation of how I made something with what I would do differently the next time I made it. This is a very important habit to get into. Improvement. Now, there very well may not be anything that you would want to change. Nothing wrong with that, at all. But if there is, this would be a suitable place to jot that down for future uses.

SAFTEY EQUIPMENT: This is overlooked way too often. Take care of yourself!

The number one item on this list is safety glasses. An Absolute Must! Ask me how I know! There was this one time several years back that I was forging. My smithy back then was in the woods. It sounds all fancy. In reality, it was just a tarp as a roof, old school. And it also was pollen season here in the NC foothills. I was constantly having grit in my eyes. To be honest, for the most part I was just used to it. I remember hammering away at the forge and doing some grinding as well with my hand crank grinding wheel. Like I said, old school. And then there was a speck of something in my eye. I did not give it much thought. I figured it would work itself out as all the other pollen specks had done. That thought went away when I woke up the next morning. That speck of something happened to be a flake of metal. Now, imagine if you will for a moment, what raw metal does outside in the fresh air, in the rain. Then imagine what raw metal does when salt water is introduced to it. Yup, that little sucker had rusted to my eyeball! And of course, as life would have it, it was on a weekend. There is nothing more enjoyable than having a special on-call eye doctor (because the Doc in a Box urgent care cannot solve this problem, I tried that) come in on a pretty Saturday morning and remove what felt like a 4x4 post that was rusted to my eye. It was really a little bitty thing, but man, that sucker turned me into a toddler. That is some next level pain right there! And, as a lesson for you all, I was NOT wearing safety glasses. So, do not be like me. Wear your safety glasses! Always! Please. Lesson learned.

Gloves. I prefer leather work gloves. For the most part, I use goat leather. They do not seem to shrink as much as others I have used in the past. The ones I use are on the thin side so I can still have some dexterity. Get them bigger than what you think. Over time, I have found that they will shrink a bit. More than anything else, do what you think is best for you. The biggest reason I use gloves is to keep my hands cleaner. Working with metal can get very grimy. They also come in handy to protect your skin from mishaps. I would not recommend non-leather gloves. Things can get hot. Non-leather can melt. To your hand. That would not be fun. Please do not do that.

Ear protection. I think this would be a personal choice. Some use it, others do not. It depends on how much noise you are making. If you think you need it, use it.

Clothing. Highly recommended. Protect your skin. I prefer natural fibers. Jeans and cotton type. Non-natural clothing can and will melt. Ask me how I know. Do not be me. *Just because it ain't red does not mean it ain't hot.* And don't forget closed-toe shoes. Please don't be that person.

While we are on the topic of safety, I would recommend you have a first aid kit close to where you are working. If you don't, that's a sure sign that you are going to need it. Burns seem to be something that happens frequently, so keep that in mind as you put together your kit.

You are going to need something to hammer on. At this level, there most likely will not be a blacksmithing type of anvil in the budget. For what we are going to be doing here, not much of a need for one either. If your vice does not have one, you can always get what is called a **bench block** or **jeweler's block**. It is just a small hunk of steel. Yes, steel please. I have seen the rubber ones. If you already have one of those, we are going to roll with it. Just remember that you may be working with hot metal and rubber will melt. If you are going to buy one, get steel- the thicker the better (at least ¾ of an inch, more if you can). I have also seen a fifteen-pound ASO (anvil shaped object) for not much more than a block. If size and room are an issue, the block will be fine. You want a stout surface to hammer on, that way you get the desired effect in your item, not in the surface.

All these tools can be acquired over time. You do not have to get everything all at once. As of this writing, the total of what you can get started is around a hundred and twenty dollars or so if everything you buy is brand new. Granted, not top of the line tools, but very serviceable. When I started out, I went to the discount tool store to get my tools to learn with. I am still using many of them to this today, ten years later. Tools will last awhile if you take care of them, no matter what the name on the side says. And remember, they are metal. Give them honor and respect. It can and should be part of your Work. They are not just a 'thing.' Take care of them and they will take care of you.

Nice To Have Tools

These will be tools that will make your co-creations much easier, maybe even "better". You may decide that some of these are on your 'need' list. There is something to be said for ease. A few of you may enjoy a more primitive approach, while others prefer not so much. So, this list may be more of a middle ground. And tempting.

Bigger Vise. You may decide that a larger vise is what will work better for you. With that said, most likely you will need a workbench to attach it to. Everyone's set up and available space is different.

Drill. You may very well have one of these. If so, bonus! They can be very handy and add a bunch of options to your work as seen below.

Wire Wheel. I am talking about the ones that will fit a drill. This can make clean-up of your work much quicker. Also, if you happen to also have a *brass* wire wheel, it can also add some color to your finished steel.

Buffing Wheel. Also, an attachment to your drill that can help shine up your work. I do not use mine a lot, but when I need it, it's really a handy thing.

Buffing, Polishing & Cutting Compound. This goes with your buffing wheel. It is like a clay or stiff paste. Experiment with the several types to see the different finishes you can accomplish. I have found that the recommended uses work the best.

Drill Bits. You are going to go through them. The two most common sizes I use are 1/8th and 1/16th. These can add a nice little hole for you to turn your work into a pendant. I have not really been able to tell much difference from the quality of the different bit makers. I usually look for a middle ground bit that is made to use on metal.

5-Gallon Bucket. This was especially useful to me in the beginning, and I still use one when I do on-the-road demos. It is an inexpensive way to store and organize all your stuff. You can keep all your tools and metal in one place. Helps with clean up as well, I think. Much less expensive than a toolbox!

Bucket Organizer. Life changer for me. I now had a place to put all my small tools and such around the outside and inside of my bucket. Helped me greatly with organization. I am one of those people that no matter what I need, it always is in the very bottom of the bucket. This was a wonderful time saver for me.

Jump Rings. To go in those nice little pendant holes you just made with your drill. I am going to leave this part up to your creativity. I have found out through vending over the years, that no matter what type, size, shape, or color of jump ring I have in, it seems to be the wrong type, size, shape, or color for that particular client and their particular preference. Here is some good news, you can now put whatever size, shape and color in just like you want it! Bonus!

Splurge-able Tools

As I have mentioned before, I started out with a very low budget, and it has grown from there. I had a hammer, the 'blacksmithing' type of a cross pein. It weighed a heavy three pounds. It didn't take me long to figure out that I did not want to swing that thing around much. I still have it though. The hammer I primarily use today is about 1.75 pounds. The other tools I got at the time were a set of pliers. One was a slip joint of about eight inches and a channel lock kind of about ten inches. Also, a hacksaw and my safety equipment. That is what I had to start learning with.

After I got back from that first week's workshop, I used the bellows I had made to make an earthen forge at home. I still have those today as well. I had a slight problem though. I did not have an anvil. I went online to price some. Nope, not happening. My very first anvil was a big rock. That lasted about an hour. It quickly became a bunch of smaller rocks. On the hunt I went. At the class, we used a bunch of odds and ends of metal. The ends of forklift forks, wheel rotors, just any large hunk of steel. I looked up steel fabricators in the area and off I went to pay them a visit. I told the man behind the desk what I was looking for and he got someone to show me around. I did not really see anything I was looking for. These were huge chunks. On the way out, I noticed what looked like a metal brick that was holding the door open. Yup, you guessed it. My very first anvil was a doorstop. I still use that very same anvil today when I do demos at festivals. That was my anvil for several years until I ran across a deal on a farrier's anvil. I got it from a fella that was getting out of the business. I used that one for many more years before I got the one that I am using currently. I guess what I am trying to say is, start where you are. As you grow, you can grow your tool selection as well. Sure, some of these will make life much easier, no doubt; not absolutely necessary though. It may also help you appreciate more the work that you do.

By now maybe you have begun to develop a metal magic practice. You might have started co-creating for others and want to upgrade from your earnings. You may already have some of these tools that you have been using for other projects. Or, you just have money burning a hole in your pocket. There is nothing wrong with being good to yourself!

I think this list might be more for the person who has gotten the "bug". The items found here can really make life easier for a budding blacksmith. However, they are totally not needed to work your metal.

Bench Grinder. This can help clean up rough ends and can shape your metal quickly. I really do not use mine much. It is very handy when I do need it though.

Bench Buffer. On one end I put a wire wheel. I do enjoy this. It really helps with clean up and polishing. I started out with the drill bit version, saw the amount of uses I had and upgraded as soon as I could. Also remember that I am in a smithy. You may very well not need to get one of these.

Anvil. At this point you may have decided that you are past the craft stage and have moved into the serious hobby stage. And you might have decided that this can even be a way to support your hobby. Anvils come in a lot of shapes, sizes, and weights...and costs. This will really depend on what type of work you are doing and would like to do. Your needs could be much different from mine. I would recommend taking your time doing some research on what others, who are doing what you want to do, use for their work. Ask what they started out with. What they would do differently. What they like about what they have and what they do not like. I think there is no 'best' anvil; there is best for you. So far this has happened on three separate occasions for me. None were new. Currently, I am using a German-style double horn. Remember, humans have been doing metal work for quite a few days now, so perhaps you can find a pre-owned one that is perfect for you.

Rotary tool. (Dremel is one of the popular brands.) If you have one of these, it can take the place of a lot of other tools. It has all kinds of different attachments. I know folks who swear by them. I do not really use one much, but we will talk about some ways to use it during the project part. If you plan to continue this craft inside a small footprint like an apartment or other limited space, this very well may be worth the investment to you. It can be a cleaner, buffer, cutter, engraver, drill and more, all in one.

Project Inception

My goal with the projects section is to show you that you do not need a lot of space nor fancy tools to get your metal magic on. It may take some patience and even some trial and error. You may want to try and get the mechanics down and then go back and start with the F.L.O.W. exercises. I am going to leave the details up to you on the when and the how's. If it were me, and I was just starting, I think I may want to make a few 'play' pieces. Or at least, get the metal prepped as much as I could beforehand. Get it to the point of where I was going to apply a sigil or writing or such. Then do the F.L.O.W. and see what becomes of it. The process of preparing your metal for work can be a wonderful time for an introduction. You could use it to get to know each other. Explain what you need or are looking for. Once again, if you are doing it this way, I would keep personal ideas generic. Little to no specifics. Just share your thoughts and the 'why' you are doing what you are doing. Think of it as sharing your story.

Action Step As you prepare to work on your project/s, write down some intentions you might want to incorporate into your pieces. Remember tools/weapons can be both offensive (think prosperity, courage, etc) and defensive (protection, deflection, etc).

INCITE

The "incite" pendant and ritual were both intense in the best way possible. I am so thankful to have been able to welcome this energy into my practice. M.W.

Below is an example of how one pendant design was created, the Work that happened before the Work, so to speak. Hopefully this will inspire you as you begin your project work.

'Incite' was a talisman that was created after a particularly disturbing supreme court decision that had many Americans feeling helpless and angry to say the least. The talisman was made on a new moon with what I call 'batch forging,' special forged items for a particular focus to a group of people. This is the article that was first posted on my blog:

My Beloved and I went away for a day to get some 'us' time for our Anniversary. And low and behold 'It' happened. The news of the US Supreme Court ruling hit. I had a feeling it was coming soon. Still, until it is 'official', it is not. Now it is official. To be honest, we started getting riled up and then decided, that for the next 24 hours (us taking our trip) we would stay off social media and focus on us. Couples care. And now here we are, back to reality so to speak. On our return, we stopped in a small town and had brunch. There it began. Over some tasty vittles, we created what we are calling 'INCITE'. It is created to be used as a talisman.

As we started discussing and dreaming into what we wanted and needed, we found these thoughts to be remarkably similar. For this Working, I have enlisted my Beloved's help with it. For many reasons. You see, she is extremely intelligent and has a depth of knowledge into areas I do not. She can see my blind spots easily. Has a great working knowledge of the Ogham. She also happens to be female and has a vastly distinct perspective on all 'this'. She will be adding her thoughts as we get into the Ogham.

I needed to do 'something'. And what I happen to do best is metal magic. There needed to be some action. While we are about action, I want to take a moment and speak to that. For me I like to focus on controlling the controllables. If I cannot change something, I look to see what I can change. What do 'I' have control over and focus on handling that. I got this thought that ran through my mind as I was thinking about this. 'Are you gonna' do something? Or just stand there and bleed?' (Great line from the movie Tombstone). For the front, or the back depending on how you want to wear it, it has three spears chiseled in. They are pointing in different directions. I see this as there being multiple types of action to be done. Action! It's just not one action item. Multiple spears for multiple action items. The spears are also crossed, which adds to a level of protection, guarding. The one in the center is above the others. You! There is ONE thing that you can do and will do. I have two mental pictures that I envision with this forging. One, a mustered host. 'The mighty Morrigan, whose pleasure was in mustered hosts', ODRAS From the Metrical Dindshenchas. It is about a group of people with sameness of mind. Joining together with a singular focus. A mustered host! And two, 'There is over his head shrieking / A lean, nimble hag, hovering / Over the points of their weapons and shields: / She is the grey-haired Morrigu' from the The battle of Magh Rath. It's about action. Together. Unified. These are the thoughts and emotions I will be using as I forge the front of this.

Let me be clear. I am angry. Almost a white heat furious. I feel betrayed by a country I served, and still serve to this day. I see dominoes falling in a direction I do not like. In my bones I feel the wrongness of it. One does not have to be female to have righteous rage about this. I have a wife. I have daughters. I am enraged to the point that tears are streaming down my face. This is me acting. This is my WORK! My Work is providing others the tools for them to do their Work. And make no mistake, this is a tool fitting of magnificent work. Weapons are not just sharp pointy things.

Now, let's get to the back of the talisman and the Ogham part. The following is written by my beloved.

Hey everyone. Sam asked me to chime in with my interpretation of our Ogham stack 'Incite'. To set the stage, here's what I experienced during the magical discussion he mentioned above: The time for weeping in silence is done. Take respite from your madness (rage) and heal your wounds. Gather your strength, nourish your body, summon your courage, and prepare to turn that grief and anger, the outrage, into ACTION. You are ready.

The feda we chose are Ceirt (Quert), Ailm and Ruis. These are NOT fluffy bunny let's-all-hold-hands-and-sing energies we are tapping. This combination is not for the faint of heart and is not to be used lightly or casually. It is a 'Ready, Aim, Fire' mustering of the troops, or your spirit. (BTW, all references to 'battles' etc are metaphorical.)

Ceirt: READY. 'a shelter of a wild hint' or lunatic. This gives us a place to settle our rage or madness, a place to order the chaos into something we can use. Connection with the Energies beyond the mists can help quiet our minds so we can prepare to fight. It is a place of 'healing, restoration, renewal and nourishment' (Daimler), so it reminds me of that place of 'Fulacht na Mór Ríoghna,' where Irish warriors would gather to rest, eat, clean their weapons, and prepare for the next battle.

The tree associated with Ceirt is apple. Beyond obvious nourishment, apple is also often used in divination, so it represents that connection to Divine voice or Direction from Deity, Ancestors, etc. It is said that Merlin, when in a fit of madness, would sit under an apple tree. Madness can lead to powerful magic if the chaos can be focused into a direction. That's what I envision Merlin doing while taking that respite, riding the wave of lunacy until it is contained, readying himself for the next magical battle.

We all have been feeling that chaos of late, haven't we? And the recent happenings in the US especially can either lead us down into full madness or incite us into action. (In this I am not talking about mental illness; please seek professional guidance if you need it.)

Ailm: AIM. Inception, 'beginning of a calling'. That pause between the death of something and the birth of something new. The rush of 'epiphany... the a-ha moment', where your purpose becomes clear and you are inspired to take action, to move forward. This fid represents Awen to me, that Breath of Spirit that breathes life into all things. It feels very initiatory, a beginning, on the threshold of something life-changing and powerful.

If you've ever shot an arrow, a 'pause while you aim' concept will be familiar to you.

This space, or pause in time, can feel like an eternity sometimes, when it's usually only a split second, albeit a very important one. It's the inspiration between thoughts and actions, the bridge between the righteous rage (or crippling grief) and the movement toward action. A lot of magic and divine direction can happen during this moment. Allowing that Hand to help us aim is stepping into the initiatory cauldron of inspiration.

This moment of epiphany can feel like terrifying elation, as contradictory as that sounds. When all the (chaotic) pieces fall into place and you suddenly realize the purpose of this moment and your sovereign place in it. The chaos is now channeled and ready, the arrow is aimed.

Ruis: ACTION. Redness, glow of anger. This is the fid of action, the loosing of the arrow. Ruis is that 'fire in the head' frenzied passion that can be powerfully positive, or totally devastating if out of control. But remember we have taken the time to ready ourselves and aim our energy, guided by our Divine helpers.

Remember that scene in Blade Trinity, when Abigail's friends have been brutally slaughtered and she is paralyzed, curled in a ball of grief and anger. Blade incites her to 'Use it. Use It. USE IT!' She screams a primal scream and It. Is. On. The righteous battle begins, the arrow shoots straight and with deadly force. This is Ruis in aimed action.

I imagine the red-streaked face of a warrior in the midst of battle. Strength was gathered in Ceirt, when we were making ready. Courage during Ailm, when our initiatory purpose was made clear and our aim steady. Now we don't have to fear losing control, as our fury is now directed toward justice.

Again, this collection of feda is not to be used lightly. Remember actions beget consequences. I think it's time others remember that too.

Sam here: I would like to leave you with a final thought that helps me in times of challenges. It is a line from the Second Battle of Moytura. 'And you, Morrígan,' said Lug, 'what power?' 'Not hard to say,' she said. 'I have stood fast; I shall pursue what was watched; I will be able to kill; I will be able to destroy those who might be subdued.'

I selected a single length of metal that I cut down to four smaller sections. Then I placed the metal on my altar until I forged it. I hope this gives you some ideas about how to start some of your work with metal magic. What stands out about the process? Can you spot the FLOW?

Projects

As you get comfortable with working with metal, you can always do your Work on certain days. I have been known to do some intense work on the moon cycles. You can also do some serious work on the High days as well, Solstice and Equinoxes. No need to limit yourself. This is your magic, your Work. You do you.

Let's keep things simple to start. With that thought in mind we are going to begin by working with copper. Before starting this or any other project, don't forget to put on your safety equipment. I have found that if you do not put it on before you start, you may forget it until after you need it. Which by then is obviously too late. Do not be that person.

I have found that working with copper is an excellent way to get into metal magic. It is well suited to folks who do not have a lot of space or tools to dedicate to the craft. And to top it off, it is just a lovely metal to work with overall. Many of the participants who come through the Immersions really enjoy working with copper. There is just something warm and welcoming about collaborating with it.

Design Ideas

As you start thinking about a possible design for your item, I would suggest that you start thinking in straight lines and dots (chisel and punch – from the tools list). What shapes are just straight lines? There are a lot in our alphabet (X – this is also multiply, marks the spot etc.), the divide symbol, an asterisk and so much more. You can use your punch to make dots to create a simple picture. What thoughts come to you? Get creative with it.

Copper Bracelet. [Tool list: tape measure, string, marker/grease pencil, vice, hacksaw, SAFTEY EQUIPMENT, file and/or sandpaper, pliers, torch, quench tank and water, solid surface, hammer, chisel, punch]

We are going to use copper pipe. As you shop for copper pipe to use for these projects, try your best to stay with the 'L' type. The walls are a little thicker than the 'M' type, so there is more copper to it. It will be a bit heftier. For this we're going to use a ¾ inch pipe. This means the pipe is ¾ inches across (in diameter). An alternative is ordering a copper plate online and cutting it to the size you want. The copper plate is technically simplest, although I find a certain satisfaction in doing a bit of work to get the metal the way I want it. Once again, you do you.

You first need to figure out the size of your wrist. Measure it around with a tape measure. If you are using a ruler, use a piece of string or something of the like to mark your wrist around. Then measure that with the ruler. Once you have the size of your wrist, **subtract** an inch. This will be the length of the ¾ inch pipe you will need to cut. And again, this is how I do it. You may need to experiment with the sizing to get what you want. I have been doing this long enough to know that everyone likes the fit differently. You may want it looser or tighter. This should be a good starting point for you to figure out how to do yours, if this is not to your liking. A small side note- it is much easier to cut more off if it is too long, than trying to glue bits back on from being too short. Ask me how I know.

Mark your pipe with your marker of choice (pencil, permanent marker, grease pencil etc.) and put it in your vise so the mark is an inch or so to one side. The side will vary depending on which hand you are going to use to cut it. I am right-handed, so I will have the mark on the right side of the vise. Now use your hacksaw to cut it at the mark. (If you happen to have a pipe cutter, you could use that as well. I did not list that as a tool because I do not think it is worth the cost. My 2 cents). Once it is cut, use your file or sandpaper to take off any burs and rough edges. No need to spend a lot of time on this. Just make it to where it is not uncomfortable to touch, and you think it's safe to handle.

You now have two options on how to continue. Option one is to drive on and use the pipe as is to make your bracelet. Option number 2 is to cut your pipe lengthwise and possibly get several thinner bracelets out of it. This is one of the main reasons I mentioned the type L copper pipe. It will be more work up front, but you will also get a lot more material to work with. To me it is worth it. Try both and then make up your mind. If you are using the copper plate, this will not need to be done.

For option number one, you are going to need to anneal your section of pipe at this point. This will help make your copper 'soft' and much more manageable/pliable. To do this you need to heat your pipe with the torch. After it has reached a high enough temperature, quench it in water. I prefer to hold it at one end with a pair of pliers, one side inside the pipe and one on the outside so you are only holding a single section. Not all the way across or around the pipe. How do you know when it's the right temperature? First, start with a clean shiny pipe. It will go through some color changing and eventually reach a dull gray color. If you heat it till it glows red, you have gone too far. This should be enough to do the trick. When it does reach this color of a dull medium to dark gray, you will quench it in water to cool it off. **An important word of caution here. Make sure the pipe opening is pointed away from you. Water will shoot through the top of it. You do not want to get splashed by this water.** Ask me how I know.

After it has cooled down (which should be very quick after a dunk), you can use the solid surface of your choice (the anvil that you have) and flatten your pipe with the flat side of your hammer. It shouldn't take too much effort to do this. If it does, you may have not gotten it hot enough. So, fire up your torch and give it another go. From time to time, I still must reheat it to get it hot enough. I get impatient. Make sure you have patience with yourself. You are learning something new. It is a process. Experiment and make sure you log your steps in your journal. That way, next time you will know what you need to do. Once you have it flat to the point it looks like just a single piece of metal, you can either continue with the 'practice' or move on to the F.L.O.W steps. Remember the W is where you do your Work.

For the second option, cut the pipe longways so you have more copper to work with. You may find that the thickness is plenty for what you need. You will need to cut it first before heating and annealing. Clamp it in the vice and use your hacksaw to cut through one side of the pipe. Or if you have a rotary tool, you could use that. Once that is done, then you can heat and quench as described. After quenching, use your pliers to open the pipe. You may have to heat a few times until you get the hang of it.

After it starts to open, you can use your hammer to finish flattening it out on the anvil. There should be about 2+ inches of material. At this point, you have multiple options.

I think one of the advantages to this style is you have a little more control over the width of it. You can use the full amount, cut it in half or even into thinner widths.

For both options: Now that you have your bracelet blank, it's time to get creative. Take the marking pencil of your choice and draw out your design. After you are settled with it, take your chisel and/or punch and start hammering in your design. There may be some trial and error here, and where a practice piece may come in handy. This may be helpful so that you can get used to how everything feels as you work it. Don't forget your ball pein hammer. The ball end makes a great texture and gives it a 'hammered' finish. After you get your design laid in, start working on the shape. A quick note about working with copper. It is what is called a 'work hardened' material. Simply put, the more you work on it, the harder it will get. At this point, if it is not fairly easy to bend and shape with your hands, you will need to anneal it again. Just heat it up and quench it.

Now you can get to cleaning. Or not. Some people (raises hand) find the worked and tarnished look of copper appealing. There may even be a nice patina to it. To me it has that antique or old look. At any rate, if you want it all shiny like a new penny, you can do that. If you happen to have a rotary tool or drill with a wire brush, easy. Go to it. If not, it's still easy. Start by giving it a good dish soap and water cleaning. Dry it off and take a fine sandpaper (maybe 800 grit to start) and sand it until you get it the way you would like it. Start with light pressure. It will just take a little time to get it all spiffy. This is just part of the process. It is also an excellent time to continue your relationship building as you are doing this. As you are cleaning, you can be thinking and talking about what it is going to be and for what it is going to be used. Now you can simply bend it with your hands to fit your wrist. Keep in mind that as you wear it, it will get stiffer, and I have found that it settles in so to speak.

After you have it all shaped and shiny, you can stop here. Or you can give another type of finish that I call flame kissing. It will involve your torch and you will also need your pliers. A quick note about using pliers. Pliers have little groves in them. The groves or teeth are there to help grip what you are holding. If you hold on too tightly, you may very well mark your metal. Something to keep in mind and to watch out for. No need for a death-grip. It is easy to sand or wire-brush out. Hold it at one end and move the flame of the torch back and forth over your bracelet. This will take a little practice. The colors will appear rather quickly. You start with a goldish shade; it moves rapidly to a reddish to a purple and if you go too far, a light silver gray. If you get to this point, you will need to start over. Just clean it off, brushing or sanding, and give it another go. No worries. I do not quench after this. I just let it cool naturally. You may want to practice this flame kissing with a separate piece to get used to the process. Keep in mind that each piece of metal will color differently. At least this has been my experience.

And there you have it. You have followed all the steps and gone with the F.L.O.W. You have yourself a magical metal tool. You can cure it over a little smoke of your choice, or not. Although it will not rust, a light coating of special oil will not hurt it. You can dedicate it as you see fit or feel free to use the ritual discussed below.

Copper Pendant- If making a bracelet sounds a little intimidating at first, feel free to start with this pendant project, which uses similar techniques. Cut the desired size from your copper sheet. If you are using a pipe, cut and flatten as described in the copper bracelet description. The wonderful thing that I like about these is you can make up a lot of them with a small amount of copper. You can have different ones for various occasions and needs. You can even make them to a specific size and use them as a notion. (I will discuss notions in the steel projects section.) And as also mentioned in the bracelet bit, you can have a variety of finishes to go with them. You can have a design, a sigil, a symbol and the list can go on. Super versatile. Your limit is your imagination. One thing you will want to add is a hole for your jump ring. This is where the drill or rotary tool comes in handy, as well as the center punch. Use the center punch to mark where you want the hole. It will make drilling much easier. I make the majority of my holes an eighth of an inch to accommodate most jump rings; of course, you can make yours whatever size suits you best. After you drill your hole and sand down the rough edges, you can flame kiss or finish as described above. Put a jump ring through it and you are off to the races. Although I have not done so, I know people who make these small and use them for earrings. We could discuss all the ways to use copper for some time. As I said earlier, use your imagination.

We are now moving into the realm of steel. Not near as easy to work with in the same way as copper, yet I think can be very fulfilling. There will be 'limits' to it as far as shaping. As you begin, please keep your mind more on marking or adding an uncomplicated design into it. This in no way makes it any less powerful. At all.

Steel Pocket Notion- In my quest to have metal more involved in my daily spiritual practice, I designed these nifty little knickknacks. I call them Pocket Notions. 'Pocket' because I wanted them small enough to fit in my pocket. Easy enough, providing you have pockets. And with them being the size & weight they are, (the ones I make are about ¼ inch thick and an inch square) I notice them, drawing my attention and focus as I go through my day, remembering why they are there and being able to feed them energy. 'Notion' to me encompasses several things: a belief or idea, and a small useful item. Hence the Pocket Notion. I like the simplicity of the sigils. To me they are primal. Sometimes (most of the time) less is more. I use them as a defined or narrow focus. Thinking of the K.I.S.S. principle (Keep It Simple Sam). I have used them just as they are. Fresh forge bling right from Her smithy? Yes please! Or clean them up and temper them to add great colors to them. I have also amplified them by using ritual. Let's begin, shall we?

For pocket notions I like them to be square. If you prefer a different shape, go for it. Find yourself a section of steel flat bar. If you are not sure of the size you would like, I would suggest visiting a big box store to see what strikes your fancy. As I stated before, I like mine to be on the bigger size. I want them to be noticed by me. As I notice it, I can 'feed' it if you will. It helps keep it in my mind. Think of it as a magical worry stone. Except without the worry part. And the part about it being a stone. So, that might not be the best example. Anyway, I like to do all my working with it while it is in bar form. In other words, one of the last things I do is cut it down to pocket notion size. It is just easier to work with in a longer form. Feel free to do what works best for you.

If you have not noticed by now, I am a fan of the hammered look. So, before I work on any design, I will take my ball pein and hammer texture the area I will be working with, with the ball side of the hammer. This can be done on the cold metal. In bar form, you can work along the three sides and edges. This just leaves the one side to do after you cut it. You should not have to hit it hard to see a dent. Do this all over the piece, overlap a little. What I mean is, if I am going to cut at an inch, I will hammer at least 1 1/4th inches of the length of the bar. That way when I get to the point I am ready to cut it, some of it will already be hammered. After the texturing, chisel in your design. Now, be easy with yourself. If you have already worked with the copper, this is not going to be anything like that. Steel is tough and hard. You may not be making very deep marks. It is ok. If you can see them, they will show up. If you have a rotary tool or an engraver, you could always try that. Remember, be patient with yourself! If you have never done this before, it does take time to get the hang of it. It is a practice. It does take just that, practice. Once you are satisfied with the look of your hammering and your design, cut it to size with your hacksaw. You are cutting steel; it may take a few minutes.

Now that you have it cut, take your ball pein and finish the cut edges you just cut. You may need to take your file or sandpaper and to get any burrs off. You have several finish options at this point. You can leave it raw or seal it with some oil, or you can even temper it to add some color. No matter what you decide, you will need to clean it. Get your sandpaper (or rotary tool or drill with a wire brush) and clean it up real good. The color should be more silver than dark gray. Once you are here, you can stop. You can cure it with smoke and then dedicate it as you see fit. If you want to temper it, hold an edge with your pliers and heat it with the torch. After a brief time, (I'm talking a minute) you will see it start to turn yellow gold, straw like color. Keep heating it and it will continue getting darker until it goes to a purple to a dark blue to a light blue to a whiteish gray. Whichever color you like, stop when it reaches it. The light blue is your limit to the temper colors.

If you want to protect it, you will need some oil of your choice (olive, canola, whatever you have handy). You'll need an old rag. You can heat seal your piece by heating till it gets to around the gold stage of temper and dab some of the oil on with the rag. This will be hot, so be careful. The oil should smoke. This is the thought behind cast iron cookware. You are creating a seal. If you have tempered your piece for the coloring, heat sealing may remove the temper colors you just got (don't lose your temper!). So I would recommend just a light coat of oil in that case.

Keep in mind that steel will rust. It is the nature of steel; it is what steel does. If you keep it sealed or if you make sure it stays dry or at least a light coating of oil, you should be fine.

Steel Pendant- As for this one, most of the how-to work, will be the same as your pocket notion. There are a few things you may want to add. I have found that a lighter steel is more comfortable and may very well be easier to work. You will need to drill a hole in it in order to hang it as a necklace. This is where a jump ring would come in super handy unless you have another idea in mind. I have also found that the tempered look is all kinds of nifty. You may even want to add a light coat of spray enamel. (I have only used the spray enamel for hair wands. I just figured it was a polite thing to do instead of raw steel in someone's hair. Everything else I leave it as is. I personally do not like a barrier between me and my metal.) The metal will change; it is in its nature. When it does, I can simply clean it back up to the raw state and do it over, or just roll with it. I have had steel items for years that have not changed much. Keep it dry and keep a light coat of oil on it. I have also found that by wearing it against my skin, the natural oils seem to help with it as well. Try several ways and see which works best for you.

Something Different

If you are wanting to create something and you are finding it a challenge for whatever reason, to cut your metal, an option that may interest you are washers. You can find them in a variety of sizes, both steel and copper. You can do something as simple as mark it with a chisel. Or engrave. Loop a leather cord through the hole and boom, pendant. Or it can be a pocket notion. These can be found almost anywhere and can be both steel and copper. Word of caution. If you get the steel kind, most are galvanized. **Don't heat those**. They may produce a toxic smoke. I recommend using washers only for designs.

Ritual

*The ritual included to charge [the metal] felt
extremely powerful. Jessica G*

I realize that everyone may be coming at this from a different place, background, or tradition. And that is perfectly fine and totally expected. As a result, I would like to offer an idea or two on some ways that you may want to honor your co-creation. If this does not speak to you, feel free to do something that does (or not). I am just simply sharing my experiences and what works for me. You do you. If I am creating something magical, I am doing it in ritual space. I have also found that doing work on the distinct phases of the moon to be interesting and effective as well. Something you may want to experiment with.

All my Work happens at Her smithy. I say Her smithy because it has been dedicated to Her, The Morrigan. I also like to set sacred space when I do Work. It sets a framework and an intention for what I am doing. For me, it's important to do this for those items that have a particular magical purpose. I feel that it greatly enhances the finished product.

Here is an example of what that may look like:

Land Spirits – (offering at Her shrine) – *"Spirits of this land, spirits of this place, I honor you now. Please accept this offering as a token of my good faith. I ask you to grant me your blessing for sacred forge work today."*

I then place a copper spear I made at Her shrine.

Back at the Smithy (which is just a few steps away) I sain the forging space – I use creek water or whiskey.

Alignment/meditation - *(Sith co nem, Nem co doman– Peace to [the] heaven[s], Heaven to [the] world / earth* (8)– this is from Her peace prophecy) I say this multiple times over and over. It helps settle my mind.

Ward – I set my container (circle) with the pillars. I have forged my representation of them and each one is placed in the rafters of the smithy. Yes, I know pillars are not usually hung from the rafters. This works for me, and they are always there, and I am not running into them or tripping over them. Win-win.

*North- *I call upon the Stone of Destiny. I have the integrity and sovereignty to call on this power to do my work. The pillar is set!*

.* West- *I call upon the Dagda's Cauldron. With hospitality I hold the bond of kinship with all beings, plant, animal, human, and Otherworldly. The pillar is set!*

*South- *I call upon the spear of Lugh. Nothing will stand against my work this day. The pillar is set!*

*East - *I call upon the sword of Nuada. I am committed to the success of this work. The pillar is set!*

(offregil drig don caath – Kings arise to battle) (9)

Then I do an invocation to the Morrigan. I will not share that here; I hope you understand.

Then before forging, I pull two Urban Crow Oracle cards (https://crowtarotshop.com/) for additional focus.

Then I go to Work.

Afterwards I clean up. Do not overlook this step. It is especially important. The tools you will be using can be hazardous. So, at the end of your time with them, show respect, clean them up and put them away. Not only will you know where to find them when you need them, it will help prolong the life of your tools. Collect any anvil dust or metal shavings for later use. Then release the container and give thanks.

Activating the Metal Magic

I do not do this for every item I make. This act is reserved for those extremely special tools. I see this as a very big deal. I cannot stress this enough! It is an oath. It is also a lifetime commitment from which one is not divorced. For me, doing something like this, seems to 'wake up' and attune the metal to what the desired need is.

Use the following, or use it as an example for which you can create your own.

Cleanse, ground and set sacred space in whatever way works for you.

Place the talisman in the palm of your non-dominant hand.

Touch the metal with the pad of the pointer and middle fingers of your dominant hand.

Close your eyes and feel your pulse pounding through your fingers, through the metal and into your palm.

Now envision the pounding of your pulse becoming the ring of a blacksmith hammer.

Now say, "I name you (_____), a weapon of warriors. For it is told that spirits may speak from weapons when weapons are worshiped by us and given proper tribute. Speak, speak, speak, I now lay the power of speech in this weapon. May you only speak the truth. You now hold the surety of truth for the actions I do in service of this bond. Metal never lies. So be it."

Allow the hammering to strike into the metal your sacred intention: the action you will take.

Once that is complete, your talisman or tool is now charged and uniquely connected to you, ready for service.

Allow the hammer to once more become your pulse and open your eyes.

Close your ritual space according to your tradition.

Talisman/tool may be recharged in this manner whenever you need it.

Action Step - What else have you created in ritual spaces? What other things have you dedicated to your work or practice? How can you incorporate this into your metal work?

Some Possible Additions to Ritual

---

*To preserve the relationship and because she asked
me to with ritual. I have a specific oil and elixir I
use that is linked to the other crowd that I work
with.* Phronesis

Here are a few additional things that you may want to
do with your metal work.

Remember steel and iron rust! Copper will also
tarnish or patina. You may want to protect them. There
are several ways to do this. It really depends on what
you are going to use it for. I have made a set of land
wards that I just left naked steel. For me, part of the
magic with this particular forging is the rust. Having
it run down and back into the earth. Full disclosure, it
was what the wards wanted; I cannot take credit for
that one. A good item to protect your metal from rust
is oil. Take your pick- olive, sunflower, corn, vegetable,
you get the idea. This works very well if your item will
be mostly indoors or worn. Every so often you can wipe
it clean and offer it your time by just being with it and
giving it a fresh coat of oil. Simply wipe on and wipe
off the excess. It is also a great way you can offer tribute
to your metal. And the oil you use can help with that if
you want. I do not want to get all out in the weeds with
this, but you could even infuse the oil you use with
herbs. I have a friend that makes woad infused oil that
I use for my work. A note on using oil, just a little dab'll

do ya. If your metal is cold (room temp), just use a light coat. If you want to take it up a level, you can 'seal' it (think cast iron cookware). You will need to heat it and then apply the oil. You want the metal hot enough so the oil 'smokes' some. Fancy wording: that is when the Polymerization happens, and it creates that non-stick surface. This option would be good if you wanted your steel to be mainly outdoors. It will offer some protection from rust. Notice I said some. Steel will rust. It is what it does. This will also 'blacken' your metal as well. Keep this in mind if you want to keep your metal raw or if you have a temper color to it, do not heat it. You will need to find the smoking point of whatever oil you decide to use. It could be as low as 325 degrees up to 500 degrees. You simply place your item in the oven and let it sit at that temp for a minimum of 30 minutes. Take your item out and use an old cloth, dip it lightly in the oil and carefully rub the oil on it. You can dab the cloth in the oil and just wipe. I would recommend holding the metal with a set of pliers so you don't burn your hands. If it smokes, you are good to go. If not, you may want to increase your temperature and give it another 30 min. Repeat until you get a good smoke, and the steel turns black. I will say that most people don't take this step. Also keep in mind, it will smoke. If you are doing this indoors, plan accordingly. As I said earlier, if you are keeping it inside mostly and you take care of it, it should not rust on you. There are entire conversations and thought processes on how 'best' to seal metal. One thing I have learned about blacksmithing- ask 5 blacksmiths a question and you'll get about 27 different answers! For my magical metal work, a good light coat of oil every now and then, is more than sufficient.

I think this would be a suitable time to talk about tribute. It is an important tidbit that should not be glossed over. To assure that we are thinking the same, here is the definition I am using for *tribute* from Merriam-Webster: *something given or contributed voluntarily as due or deserved, especially a gift or service showing respect, gratitude, or affection.* I would like to unpack a passage that we looked at earlier in the Lore section:

'*After the battle then the champion Ogma found Orna, sword of Tethra king of the Fomorians. Ogma unsheathed the sword and he cleaned it. Then the sword recounted everything it had done, because it was the way then when unsheathed [for swords] to reveal the actions they had done. Because of that legacy swords are given the tribute of cleaning them. Further, spells have been kept in swords since. And the reason demons used to speak through weapons then is that they were worshipped by people and weapons were among the sureties [116] of the time.*'

I notice right at the start that the sword has a name that was known at least to Ogma. Then the first thing that was done was to clean the sword after unsheathing. That seems to me to be the *tribute*. And to me, it is also much more than simply wiping it down. In my mind I picture that the cleaning had a ritualistic feel to it. I know when I was in the Army and we 'cleaned' our weapons, it was a tad bit thorough. They were disassembled, cleaned, inspected, a little oil applied, reassembled, another wiping of oil, inspected and then a final inspection. I am doubtful this was the exact same process for Ogma; it does give me some thoughts as to how to visualize it as a complex series of steps meant to show respect through time and attention given.

I can see Ogma sitting off to the side a bit, alone with Orna. Everything gathered to give a good cleaning-some water, rags, a good stone for sharpening and oil for final coating. I can see him starting with the sheath and giving it a good once over and general cleaning as an introduction of himself to Orna. Once that is done, he takes Orna out of the sheath, inspecting and giving it the once over making a mental note of where some additional time may be needed. Pours some water over the hilt and uses a rag to wipe it clean and dry. Repeats as needed. Does the same along the blade. Uses the stone to work out any nicks and to apply a fresh edge. Takes the oil to give it all a light coat for protection. All the while he is doing this, I can imagine Ogma telling Orna stories and marveling at the sword's appearance and details of its craftsmanship. Then after all that, is when Orna gave its recounting.

I have come to appreciate and even look forward to my time in tribute. I do this for all the metal items that I have for any type of magical working. From the candle dish all the way to the athame. Copper and steel alike. To me it is not a chore; I look forward to it. I am sure some of that is due to me co-creating the items. Some of it may be due to the relationship I have created with each by offering the tribute. Now, I am not saying that every time I give tribute to my incense holder it starts to run off at the mouth. (And for the record, as of this writing, it has not been named by me.) Not at all. I am saying that I have respect for my incense holder that aids me in my Work, and I want to give deference to that. So, I encourage you as you co-create (or acquire) metal items for your Work, give tribute to them. I know for me it has made a tangible, noticeable difference in all my Workings. Do not take my word for it, give it a go yourself. Pick one item and start from there. Keep a record of your interactions. I am referring to the F.L.O.W. that we discussed. 'Work' can also mean the Work you do with your metal item or tool.

Action Step - Do you have any tools that you work with that you give tribute to? Why? What is the relationship like between you? Are there any tools that you are now looking at differently?

Something else to think about is what I call Curing your work. At times when it is asked of me, I will smoke cure my Work. It is simply using wood and burning it, so it smokes. Think of it as infusing the tree energy into your Work. This is also a great way to honor the Work you are wanting to do with your piece. Now, it doesn't take much wood; I am not talking about a bonfire, although there is nothing wrong with a good fire. I think you could use a charcoal disk like you use for incense. Just shave some wood and sprinkle on the disk. As it smokes, hold your metal over it. The wood you use is up to you. On rare occasions, customers have sent me wood to use for them. Otherwise, I only use what grows around here and has been gifted to me. I have not had to harvest any yet. These are some ways I use woods that are local to me, and it should be enough to give you some ideas and give you a good start. And before we get into it, yes, I know these can be used other ways or they may mean such and such to so and so. This is currently how I use them and what works for me. Remember when we started this journey together, and I mentioned that I grew up in the mountains of Western North Carolina? I grew up with these trees. As a child and young adult, these trees were my friends. I played amongst and in these trees. I know them by their leaf and bark and understand some of their stories. I say all that to say, while I am far from an expert on trees, this is how I understand them from my relationship with them.

Apple- health, abundance and sustenance
Beech- memory and knowledge
Birch- Beginnings and cleansing
Cedar- Cleansing and longevity
Cherry- Sweetness and beauty
Elder- health, growth, and protection
Hemlock- joy and reassurance
Hickory- durability and character
Holly- protection, cheeriness, purity
Locust- permanence, boundary, protection, the 'Others' as well as magic
Maple – practical, prominent, emerge
Mountain Laurel- beauty, hope
Oak- strength, toughness and wisdom
Pine- purification, health, and persistence
Poplar- practical, versatile
Rhododendron- boundary, aide, conceal
Sassafras- creative, discernment, magic

I hope this little list is helpful to you. You may very well have a different understanding of some of these. And that is ok, you may have a different relationship with them.

Another finish that you may want to think about is tempering or what I call 'flame kissing'. This works for both steel and copper and it will take some practice to get the hang of it. With copper it can produce some really lovely colors of gold, red and even purple. Steel ranges from a straw-color all the way through purple to a dark-to-light blue. I think it is worth learning how to do, and it will take practice to get it how you may want (and of course the metal will have a say so as well). For detailed instructions, see the Projects section above.

Action Steps -What trees do you have a relationship with? Are they close? What feeling do you get from them that you may want to add to your work? What are some other ways or items you may want to add to this list? What wood would you like to use in this process if any? Why that tree or trees?

Summary of Part 4

In this section we discussed various tools that are needed for this fantastic craft. The focus of the projects was more towards cutting and marking our metal. We started using what tools we have on hand and as we worked on our craft, and possibly upgraded our tool list. We discussed some projects that should be doable in any size area and got a good idea how to work with steel and copper. And hopefully by doing these, it sparked an interest or even inspiration on other projects to make with metal. I also hope your understanding of 'weapon' can now be used for both offensive (to attract something) and defensive (to prevent something) intentions. And, that they do not need to be sharp pointy things.

We then talked about setting sacred space or ritual for doing your work. And the possibility of dedicating a space for it. And we discussed adding ways to seal your work, with oils and curing with wood. I discussed some thoughts on giving your metal tribute as another way to deepen your practice.

Action Step - What differences do you notice working with the different metals? How does that reflect with how you first started to work with it during the F.L.O.W. steps? What did you learn from doing a project?

Conclusion

We have come to the end of our time together. Within these pages we have covered a lot of ground. My goal was to start laying a foundation of metal magic for you. To look at ways to incorporate it into your life as a tool and or a weapon. We did a quick study of copper, bronze/brass & iron /steel as I understand them. Talked about places where they can be found both in a retail and reclaimed area. I possibly took you on a small trip down a rabbit hole. Added a few dots to be connected. Possibly shined a light on an overlooked area. And, just maybe, it gave you a different viewpoint to absorb some interesting possibilities. I shared with you the acronym F.L.O.W. (Feel, Listen, Open, Work) that I teach as a process to deepen your learning and understanding of metal. And how to begin using metal in our magical practice. I showed you a few examples of what it has been like for me to go through the FLOW process. We discussed a few simple projects that can be done at home with minimal tools. (These have endless possibilities by the way.) I discussed some tool upgrades you may want. Safety, safety, safety! Always work safely! Proper protection and clothing. I offered a few projects to do for those that wanted to try their hand at creating their own magical tools or weapons. I am hopeful it will open a whole new world, one richly filled with different lovely metals. For adornment, for protection, for the beauty of it, and so much more!

Next Steps

Here are some next steps for you if you are so inclined. First and foremost, continue your Work. This is a Practice! So, practice. Invest time with different metals. Important - Keep a journal of your observations. Finding out what doesn't work is very valuable. Do not discount this. It happens. It is ok. It is part of the practice. It will lead to growth.

Ways to increase your relationship and understanding of your metal:

- Spend more time with it. Meditate more with it before working. Stay in the F.L.O. of the F.L.O.W. steps. I have been known to have an 'idea' come to mind for an item and spend months working it out. Sometimes it is before working with the metal. Sometimes it is with some of the metal. I can get a 'this needs to be made' polite suggestion and it will take time to work on it. There are times I have focused on a piece of metal for months or even a year or more before I 'got' what it wanted to be. Be patient. It is a relationship. It may not happen overnight or right away. I do think it is so worth it!

- If it is getting really good to you, and you live in or close to a larger city, see if there is a community "Maker Space". Most I have seen have space for metal working mediums. Some of them may even have blacksmithing. The one where I teach has about any craft imaginable.

They are great for learning in a safe space and may even supply tools to use while there.

- Finally, you can always take a weekend workshop here! I would be honored to be of service. Got to RavensKeepForge.com for the schedule.

Authors Note

I would like to thank you for sharing in this journey and supporting my Work. I never in a million years thought I would write a book. Nor did I want to. This book was one of those 'polite suggestions' I got after I went in search for more information on metal magic. This is probably a good spot to explain what I mean by that. If you have ever seen the movie 'Boondock Saints' this will be familiar. There is a scene at the end of the movie where in the courtroom Connor says, 'These are not polite suggestions. These are codes of behavior, and those of you that ignore them will pay the dearest cost.' Hence, I use that term when I am 'asked' to do something by the Morrigan. She gives me a 'polite suggestion'. And here we are.

It is my great hope that you find this book useful in your magical and personal life. Over the course of writing this book, it changed. I changed. I started out with focusing on what I do the most- forge work. And then quickly I realized it was not going to be helpful to very many people. So, I backed up and gave it another go. And again. I did this several times to get it to what you now have. I have done my best to put into words what I know and how I experience metal magic. It is my desire that no matter where you are or what you have access to, it is a practice that you can participate in. I have found it to greatly enhance my wellbeing, and it is my expectation you will have some of the same adventures.

I welcome ideas that you may have for anything you would like more information on. I believe what I have written here is an excellent introduction. And it is just that, an introduction.

Finally, I would consider it an enormous honor if you would give this Work a review. This will do a few things for me. One, I will know what you thought of it, your experience, and feelings. It will help potential readers become familiar with what this book is about. It will give the book greater visibility and a greater chance of getting found by more readers. Simply stated, your book review will help validate the worthiness of this book. After all, there is not much information on metal magic out there. We are trail blazers together!

I will personally read each of your comments and reviews; I promise you that.

Sam 'Bo' Thompson

Please follow me on

Facebook: www.facebook.com/RavensKeepForge

Instagram: www.instagram.com/ravenskeepforge

Website: www.ravenskeepforge.com

Thanks again for your support!

And as an additional way to show my appreciation, I have some bonus content for you, including instructional videos to help you with your projects. Go to www.ravenskeepforge.com/bookextras and use *MetalNeverLies* as the password. I will be adding content sporadically.

Endnotes

1. All below references are from Wikipedia Wikipedia, the free encyclopedia - https://en.wikipedia.org/wiki/Main_Page

2. Animism - Wikipedia - https://en.wikipedia.org/wiki/Animism

3. Old Copper complex - Wikipedia - https://en.wikipedia.org/wiki/Old_Copper_complex

4. 9 Signs and Symptoms of Copper Deficiency (healthline.com) - https://www.healthline.com/nutrition/copper-deficiency-symptoms

5. Iron deficiency anemia - Symptoms and causes - Mayo Clinic - https://www.mayoclinic.org/diseases-conditions/iron-deficiency-anemia/symptoms-causes/syc-20355034

6. The Fate of the Children of Turenn (maryjones.us) - http://www.maryjones.us/ctexts/turenn.html

7. (37) Early Irish Ironworking | Brian G Scott - Academia.edu - https://www.academia.edu/44050593/Early_Irish_Ironworking

8. Translated by Isolde ÓBrolcháin Carmody - https://storyarchaeology.com/author/isolde/

9. Translated by Isolde ÓBrolcháin Carmody - https://storyarchaeology.com/author/isolde/
-Cath Maige Tuired: A Full English Translation (Irish Myth Translations) by Morgan Daimler Cath Maige Tuired: A Full English Translation (Irish Myth Translations): Daimler, Morgan: 9798551167181: Amazon.com: Books

-Borsje, Jacqueline. "Omens, Ordeals and Oracles: on Demons and Weapons in Early Irish Texts." Peritia 13 (1999): 224–248. Web. <u>Omens, ordeals and oracles: on demons and weapons in early Irish texts | Jacqueline Borsje - Academia.edu</u>

Acknowledgments

I would like to thank Coral for her constant encouragement over the years and for challenging my thought processes along the way.

Mara - I am grateful for your tireless support, steadfastness and attention to detail and friendship.

TJ - for sharing my desire to learn more about metal magic and being someone to bounce 'crazy' ideas off of.

My grandparents - who are now my ancestors. They always had time for ALL my questions and taught me answers to some of life's greatest questions.

Dusty - for having faith in me at a time when I did not. And for teaching some very important life lessons. None of us are as smart as all of us. You can be right, or you can be happy. You can't be both. And perhaps the most important, 'This is my favorite!'

Arlene - for giving me the shove to write That. One. Article. Thanks for believing in me!

Beth, Amanda, and Chris - for reading the early version (mess) and giving me great feedback in ways to improve this finished book.

Tomi – for always encouraging me to live BIG.

Susannah – For your friendship and guidance over the years.

Deborah – for having all the time in the world to discuss the nuts and bolts of getting this done!

Byron – for your endless advice and loving friendship over the years.

About the Author

A tad bit about me:

I've been a practicing pagan since the 90's (does that date me or what?), past VP and President of Triad CUUPs (Covenant of Unitarian Universalist Pagans). During the years I have become a Reiki Master Teacher and a certified Great Life Coach. I learned Primitive Blacksmithing Around 2012 and took to it like a duck to water. I am honored to have been a finalist in *Our State* Magazine for a forged steel and copper rose. I teach both Primitive Blacksmithing and Magical Blacksmithing in the Foothills of NC. The focal point of my Work is on the magical part of blacksmithing and I am currently a full-time magical smith. Being a Priest of the Morrigan heavily influences what I do and the smithy is dedicated to Her. I am also a proud Army Veteran.

Printed in Great Britain
by Amazon

87051595R00100